Question Quest for Ages 8–14

The ability to ask incisive questions is a powerful skill set that children can acquire and develop if the classroom and whole-school environments support it. This essential book offers a range of engaging and inclusive activities that promotes children's questioning and feeds their natural sense of curiosity and wonder.

Question Quest explores the various types of questions that can be asked in a number of educational contexts, from the point of view of both teachers and pupils. Packed with 100 practical activities, the book seeks to boost children's self-confidence in asking questions and provides the tools to establish a 'questioning classroom' where asking questions is encouraged and celebrated in order to enhance children's learning. With clear and practical explanations, the authors argue how questioning is an intelligent behaviour that is essential in nurturing children's innate desire to learn constantly. Topics covered include:

- Establishing a questioning classroom
- Questioning and creativity
- Questions and creative writing
- Conducting a discussion
- Philosophical enquiry
- Questioning and life coaching

This book is a key resource for any school, teacher or parent looking to foster and develop critical thinking skills in children and young people.

Steve Bowkett taught secondary English for 18 years and enjoyed a 30-year career visiting hundreds of schools to work with children and deliver teacher training. He has published over two dozen educational books in the areas of literacy, creative writing, thinking skills, philosophy and wellbeing.

Tony Hitchman has worked in a variety of primary schools, teaching everything from Foundation to Year Six. He has held numerous posts, including for art, design, science and curriculum development, and has worked as a special needs co-ordinator, culminating in 11 years as a head teacher at a predominantly service school with very high levels of mobility.

Question Quest for Ages 8–14
100 Practical Activities to Build Critical Thinking and Self-Esteem Through Questioning

Steve Bowkett and Tony Hitchman

LONDON AND NEW YORK

Designed cover image: Liderina via Getty Images and © Tony Hitchman

First published 2025
by Routledge
4 Park Square, Milton Park, Abingdon, Oxon OX14 4RN

and by Routledge
605 Third Avenue, New York, NY 10158

Routledge is an imprint of the Taylor & Francis Group, an informa business

© 2025 Steve Bowkett and Tony Hitchman

The right of Steve Bowkett and Tony Hitchman to be identified as authors of this work has been asserted in accordance with sections 77 and 78 of the Copyright, Designs and Patents Act 1988.

All rights reserved. No part of this book may be reprinted or reproduced or utilised in any form or by any electronic, mechanical, or other means, now known or hereafter invented, including photocopying and recording, or in any information storage or retrieval system, without permission in writing from the publishers.

Trademark notice: Product or corporate names may be trademarks or registered trademarks, and are used only for identification and explanation without intent to infringe.

British Library Cataloguing-in-Publication Data
A catalogue record for this book is available from the British Library

ISBN: 978-1-041-00212-3 (hbk)
ISBN: 978-1-041-00207-9 (pbk)
ISBN: 978-1-003-60871-4 (ebk)

DOI: 10.4324/9781003608714

Typeset in Sabon
by Apex CoVantage, LLC

Tony – To Sue – as always.

Steve – To Wendy of course and to all the young thinkers who dare to question, challenge, doubt.

Contents

Introduction   *xii*
Using the Book   *xv*

1 Establishing a Questioning Classroom   1

Parroting 1
A Question a Day 3
Questions Around a Pencil 3
World of Wonder 4
Kinds of Questions 5
Would You Rather 7
Question Match 8
Strength of Reasons 9
Questions Around the Star 11
Leading Questions 12
Categorising Questions 13
Exemplar Questions 15
Questions Around Concepts 15
A Question of Relevance 15
Effective Learners 17
Bloom's Taxonomy of Thinking 17
Questions Around a Story 20
The Box With the Answer 20
Bloom's Taxonomy Around a Topic 23
Problems With Questioning 23
Benefits of Questioning 24
Activities to Encourage Pupil Questioning 24
Clarity of Language 25

      Ambiguous Words 26
      Reflective Questioning on Learning 26
      Picture Exploration 27
      Questioning as a Subversive Activity 29

2   Questioning and Creativity   31

      Aspects of Creativity Include 31
      Similes and Metaphors 31
      Ambiguous Shapes 32
      Ambiguous Shapes Grid 33
      Symbols 35
      Love Is 37
      Switching Domains 37
      Odd One Out 39
      CREATE 39

3   A Medley of Question-generating Activities   40

      Getting-to-know-you Questions 40
      Picture Masking 41
      What Is . . . ? 41
      Question Flip 42
      Twenty Questions 43
      A Mini Mystery 43
      Toggle 44
      What Might Happen Next? 45
      Questioning So-called Nonsense Words 45
      Kennings 47
      Bouba-kiki 48
      Question Ripple 48
      Synaesthesia 49
      What Is It Like to Be . . . ? 49
      Questions Around a Theme 50
      Thought-provoking Questions 51
      Faction 51
      Please, Mr Einstein 52
      Context Sentences 52
      Structure and Function 54
      The 'Who Am I?' Game 55

Question Wall 55
Knock On 56
The Why Game 57
Etymology 58
Using Proverbs 59
I Don't Know 64
Marooned 65
This Is the Answer – What Are the Questions? 66
Thinking Cards 66
The Computer in the Box 70

4 **Questions and Creative Writing**   72

The Counter-flip Game 72
Story Strips 75
Story Strings 76
Similarities and Differences 80
Character Thumbnails 80
Add-a-bit 82
Character Wheel 82
Viewpoints 83
Settings 84
Questioning the Answers 85
First Lines, Last Lines 86
Story Grids 87
Strength of Reasons Revisited 89
Back to the Grids 90
Story Dice 91

5 **More Challenging Activities**   92

Grid Work 92
Infoscraps 95
Rhetorical Techniques 95
Sorting for Relevance 98
Letter to the Editor 98
Debating Tactics 101
A Raft of Problems 102
Take It Further – If-Then 107
The Trolley Problem 109

Quizzing the Text 109
The Moon Cannot Be Stolen 110
Interrogate the Speaker 111
New Earth 117
Questions About Questions 119

6   Conducting a Discussion   121

The False Choice 123
Red Herrings 123
Circular Arguments 124
Use of Extreme Conclusions 124
Dissect the Question 124
Point of View 125
New Housing Development 126
Generalised Opinions 129
Assumptions and Dubious Connectives 129
Colourful Language 132
Analogies 132
Intensifiers 132
Nuances of Language 133
Summing Up So Far 133

7   Philosophical Enquiries   135

Rules of the Game 136
Getting Started 136
Testing the Limits 137
Wrestling with Abstract Concepts 137
Present the Stimulus 138
Thinking Time 138
Question Making 139
First Thoughts 139
The 'Meat' of the Enquiry 139
Philosophical Moves 140
Questions, Questions 141
4Cs 143
Sample Enquiry 143
A Note on Discovery Learning 145

8 Questions and Life Coaching   147
   Dealing With Limiting Beliefs 153
   SMART 153
   Cycle Questioning 153
   How Did It Go? 157
   Question Checklist 157

Endwords   158

Bibliography   159
Index   161

Introduction

The physicist and Nobel Laureate Isidor I. Rabi was once asked why he became a scientist rather than a doctor, lawyer or businessman like other people in his neighbourhood. His reply was, "My mother made me a scientist without ever intending it. Every other Jewish mother in Brooklyn would ask her child after school: 'Did you learn anything today?' But not my mother. She always asked me a different question. 'Izzy,' she would say, 'did you ask a good question today?' That difference – asking good questions – made me become a scientist."

Asking questions is an essential element of any child's education, but we've rarely come across any formal training in schools that not only teaches children how to ask incisive questions based on the cultivation of curiosity in young learners but also any that systematically establishes a classroom ethos where children feel they have the confidence and self-esteem to enquire in the first place. The writer and philosopher Mel Thompson, in his *Teach Yourself Philosophy of Mind*, quotes the psychologist John Dewey, who asserts that children learn best when they are presented with challenges and questions rather than being forced to learn information that has no relevance to them. An extension of this is encouraging children to ask their own questions, ideally based on ideas and problems that have personal relevance. This is a point we'll return to later.

My (Steve's) own 'question quest' didn't really begin in school until I was an A-level student. I had a deep interest in science, but I would try and satisfy my curiosity through reading at home, being too shy to ask my teachers, and also fearing that I'd be judged as stupid or ignorant by my classmates. That began to change during, ironically, an English lesson. We were studying Thomas Hardy's poem 'The Garden Gate.' After a second reading, our English teacher, Mr Roberts, asked us what we thought about it. A strained silence followed and lengthened; Pete Roberts having the good sense not to try to fill the silence by jumping in with his own view. One member of our group, a big rugby player named Dave, obviously had an opinion; he had gone red in the face, and we could see that he was bursting to say something. Pete Roberts made eye contact with Dave and held it until Dave blurted out that he thought the poem was trite and maudlin. We expected a negative reaction from Mr Roberts, but instead he nodded slowly, smiled and said, "Three months in, I'm pleased to say that I think our A-level English course has just begun."

After that, having been given permission to express our views and, by implication, to ask questions, the course became far more enjoyable and interesting. Pete Roberts had changed the nature of our classroom interactions and stated explicitly that he didn't mind silences if they were 'reflective silences', a concept that's well known nowadays as thinking time or 'wait time'. This phrase was coined by the American educator Mary Budd Rowe, who found that teachers typically waited between only 0.7 and 1.5 seconds after asking a question before supplying the answer. She also discovered that increasing the wait time to three seconds or more increased students' creativity and capacity to learn. This is especially important when children's opinions are asked for: not only must children feel they have permission to offer a view, but they need time to formulate one, for although the mind works quickly (don't think of pink elephants!), opinions also have an affective or feeling component – how we *feel* about, say, 'The Garden Gate' needs to be noticed before being expressed. The author and journalist Libby Purves has summed up this attitude as, 'It's good to know how to pause without panic, and think without confusion' (www.facultyfocus.com/articles/effective-teaching-strategies/student-learning-in-3-seconds).

Another important aspect of establishing a 'questioning classroom' is that, generally speaking, pupils' tendency to ask questions lessens as they get older. According to author Brendan Cahill, the average first grader asks 300 questions a day, while the average high school pupil asks less than three.

There are several reasons for this. One, already touched upon, is that many adolescents are more self-conscious than younger children; I (Steve) was desperately shy right through my teens and well into my 20s – heaven forbid having my classmates stare at me as I blushed deeply after daring to ask a (stupid) question – although the mathematician Alfred North Whitehead suggests that 'the "silly" question is the first intimation of some totally new development.' Another factor is the constant pressure to 'cover' the curriculum: what teacher wouldn't feel judged if they failed to deliver all of the topics in the syllabus in a given time? Unfortunately, the UK National Curriculum specifies not only 'programmes of study' but also 'attainment targets', these being checked by periodic visits by Ofsted inspectors (a controversial topic in the news as I write this), although there seems to be more flexibility for teachers now than when the NC was first introduced. And while it's reasonable for children to gain a general knowledge in a variety of subject areas, the reasoning behind this, according to Brendan Cahill, authors Neil Postman and Charles Weingartner, and educationalist John Abbott (see Bibliography), is rooted in the 'factory' or 'industrial' model of education, where the primary aim is for children to reach certain standards of literacy, numeracy *and compliance* so that young people going out into the world will make good workers and therefore more profit for shareholders, etc. or is this too strong a view? Coincidentally, as I write this introduction, the former UK Prime Minister, Rishi Sunak, announced during office his pledge to ensure Maths should be taught 'in some form' up to the age of 18, a move supported by Sam Sims, Chief Executive of National Numeracy at the time, because that would bring 'significant advantage for labour market skills and longer term economic benefits' (www.bbc.co.uk/news/education-64559118).

While we think that all children should have the opportunity to receive the best grounding possible across a range of subjects, we agree with Brendan Cahill that especially in the digital age, 'the only thing economically that seems to be rewarded is one's ability to be creative ... it is only those capable of asking the big questions and creatively finding solutions to them that will stand out and be rewarded', hence Postman and Weingartner's assertion that education should be pupil-centred with a focus on questioning and problem-solving, by which they mean real-world problems that are relevant to the pupils themselves.

There are many books on developing questioning and enquiry skills – again, look at the Bibliography. Most of them emphasise the importance of encouraging children's questioning but are rather light on practical ways of achieving this. Our aim in this book is to offer a range of techniques and activities (over 100 of them) that will not only encourage children to ask more and more incisive questions as a key aspect of their education but will also help them to become more independent learners so that, for instance, they might be inclined to check information for themselves rather than just accepting it uncritically; a theme that we also explore in our previous book, 'Understanding the World Through Narrative.' This is especially important in a world increasingly infected by mis- and disinformation, bias, outright lies, relative truths, fake news and conspiracy theories. The danger of being gullible and therefore vulnerable, and educators' concerns about this, isn't new: Postman and Weingartner's 'Teaching as a Subversive Activity' came out in 1969 and its central message is even more relevant today. The title of Chapter One is 'Crap Detecting', echoing a comment by author Ernest Hemingway who, when asked if there was one quality needed above all others to be a good writer, replied, 'Yes, a built-in, shock-proof crap detector'. We would extend that ability to include dealing with the world at large.

Using the Book

Questioning/enquiry activities are offered within a number of contexts which increase in sophistication as the book progresses. What children learn in an earlier section will be useful in later ones. Ideally then, the sections should be worked through in order as a programme of study but having said that, if any particular section takes your fancy or fits in better with your own syllabus, feel free to cherry-pick. In light of this option, we've mentioned certain points in several of the sections so that they are self-contained and can be used independently.

1 Establishing a Questioning Classroom

Parroting

This is the process of wanting students to recall and feed back information as it was presented to them by the teacher – Oxford Languages defines it as 'mechanically' repeating. The act of parroting is nothing more than a check that pupils have remembered information previously given to them. Simple recall is a low-level skill, which we'll look at again in the context of Benjamin Bloom's taxonomy of thinking skills.

Parroting does not encourage questioning, either explicitly or implicitly. It also shows itself when children are asked to copy down facts from the smartboard or a book. Steve took biology as an A-Level subject, and his zoology teacher would write on the board verbatim chunks of text from the standard textbook he was using as the basis for the course ('Animal Biology' by Grove and Newell). Then, all the students had to do was copy the same sentences into their notebooks. We're sure you will agree on what a colossal waste of time this was when the group could all have been given a copy of the book – or bought their own – and be asked to read up certain sections that they could discuss and enquire about in a subsequent lesson.

Steve has recounted elsewhere the time he was invited to run some creative writing workshops in a primary school: After break, my session was with a Year Six group. I went to the classroom about ten minutes early to get ready and found that the class teacher was still there, tidying up. She'd clearly just done a science lesson with the children because on the board she'd written, 'light travels in straight lines.' It was obvious she wanted to get away and grab a quick coffee, but I couldn't resist asking if light *always* travels in straight lines and, if not, what might affect its trajectory. She didn't know and admitted that she'd just taken the fact from a textbook. What was even more alarming was that none of the children had questioned the information but had simply copied it down in their notebooks.

Something akin to parroting exists even at the degree level. When I (Steve) was preparing to write my dissertation for a B.Ed. degree, I was told by my mentor to quote as many authorities as possible, especially if I wanted to include any original ideas of my own. I was actually advised that the more quotes I included from other people, the better my grade would be.

In its most basic and blatant form, parroting looks like this –

Teacher: London is the capital of England. (And subsequently) What is the capital of England? (We've come across the possibly apocryphal story that when asked this, one child said 'E' and got told off for being lippy!)
Class: London is the capital of England.

In a questioning classroom, the same fact can be 'delivered', but children would be encouraged to ask questions around it:

Activity:

Where does the word capital come from? (And by extension, where did the words London and England come from?)

What is the purpose of a capital?

Does a country need to have a capital?

Who decides where the capital of a country is located?

Is a country the same as a nation?

Where do the words capital, country and nation come from?

Can the capital of a country change? If so, who decides that?

When did London become the capital of England and why?

Does a place need to be a certain size to become a capital?

You (and your pupils) can probably think of even more questions around this topic. We also want to admit at this point that we don't know the answers to some of the previously stated questions. And if *you* don't, how do you feel about that? It's common in our experience for teachers to be regarded as 'repositories of right answers', but we think this attitude is mistaken. Steve remembers a tutor at university telling his group that if a child asks a question the teacher can't answer, there's no shame in it and that the most appropriate and useful reply would be, 'I don't know, but how might we find out?' (We make this point several times throughout the book.) That 'we' is important since it implies that the teacher is also a learner and is keen to discover more, thus 'modelling the behaviour' that we wish to cultivate in the children.

We think it was Somerset Maugham* who said in the context of evolving as a writer that we are all travellers on the same road: some people are farther along than others, but we are all going in the same direction. The same is, or should be, true of learning. The idea of 'lifelong learning' is common in the educational world, but we wonder how many adults are fired by the same curiosity that children, especially young children, display.

* If we can't remember who actually said a quote, we always attribute it to Somerset Maugham.

Activity: A Question a Day

Inform the class that either you or one of the children can kickstart the day by coming up with an interesting question. This helps children to become increasingly comfortable asking questions. Each day's question can be discussed or answered there and then or pinned up on a question board to be researched later. If this is the case, invite children to find out facts about the question, which are pinned up around it. You can also suggest that parents get involved by asking children what was the most interesting question they came across at school today.

'Kickstarter' questions can also invite children to reflect about themselves and their learning. So, for instance –

What is the best thing I can do to help myself today?
What am I excited about today?
What am I grateful for?
Am I nervous about anything? Why is that?

Take it Further with end-of-day questions. Ask children to swap a 'take-home question', preferably one that they don't know the answer to, but one that interests them. Children can then do some research around it as a piece of homework and, ideally, involve parents in helping to find relevant information.

Activity: Questions Around a Pencil

A quick, useful and enjoyable activity is to show children an everyday object, say a pencil, and ask them to think of as many questions as they can within a given time limit. Emphasise that neither they nor you need to know the answers to any of the questions, though subsequently you can all endeavour to research answers and also do a 'question analysis' to group the questions into categories – which we'll look at later.

During one workshop, we ran this activity and then we attempted to classify the various kinds of questions. One category was questions that have a 'right answer' but one that can never be known, such as how many pencils are in the world at this moment? We asked the class if they could think of other questions of the same type and the children came up with things like – How many pens are there in the world right now? How many erasers are in the world at this second? And so on. To us, this indicated their relative inexperience in working with questions since they were simply asking the same question but using different objects. If you find the same is true of your class, try them again when their questioning skills are more fully developed.

Activity: World of Wonder

An extension to this activity we call a 'world of wonder'. Steve well remembers a chemistry teacher in a school where he taught being truly amazed by how a radio worked (he called it a wireless, which shows how long the memory had stayed with him). It was refreshing to see such wonderment in an adult, especially since he was rather cynical about so many other things. Curiosity and wonderment go together. Taking things for granted, or not thinking about and questioning them at all, is a habit that can be changed. In the world-of-wonder activity, children are invited to look around the classroom or bring some everyday object from home, and not just to question it but to appreciate its cleverness, usefulness and originality. We remember one class marvelling over the ingenuity of a ring-pull can and another class discussing what a good idea fluorescent lights were. Hand in hand with this came a flurry of questions around these inventions and others we looked at. Taking a little time to find out more about who invented something like the fluorescent light and how it works encourages children's research skills and, again, emphasises the positive attitude of discovery that questioning embodies. The same sense of wonder can be cultivated during nature walks: as well as being taught facts about the natural world, express your own wonderment, not just in the fact that life exists in the first place, but its incredible diversity and the astonishing ways in which it works. To feel wonderment leads easily to 'I wonder' questions – I wonder where, when, what, how, who, why.

As an adjunct to what's been said, give sincere praise when children ask questions or otherwise display curiosity. Fear of being wrong or looking ignorant is a strong negative force that can militate against asking questions. We emphasise to any groups we visit that asking questions is an intelligent behaviour because it says, in effect, that 'I don't know but I'm keen to find out.' One teacher Steve worked with supplied each child in his class with coloured cards; red, yellow and green. Holding up a red card indicated that a child didn't understand something that had been said or didn't know the answer to a question. A yellow card meant that a child thought he knew or understood or was at least willing to take a guess and try to express his understanding in his own words. A green card meant that a child understood/knew the answer. We were surprised at how well the simple technique worked, as we expected many of the children would not want to admit that they didn't know. But because the classroom ethos supported questioning and 'wanting to find out more' children were comfortable with holding up red cards, these acting as useful feedback to the teacher to rephrase an idea or to encourage the class to research answers, or for green card children to share their understanding. We should also mention that the teacher too had a similar set of cards and did not feel at all self-conscious in holding up a red or yellow one.

Kinds of Questions

The first point to be made is to be aware of the ratio of teacher-initiated questions to pupil questions in any lesson. In his book 'The Practice of Questioning', Professor of Education J. T. Dillon states that classroom researchers repeatedly find 'the dearth of student questions and the deluge of teacher questions' and quotes from studies that point out the same pattern exists in both primary and secondary schools, which found that over the course of an hour, 84 questions came from the teacher and two questions from all students combined in the class and that over the school year, one question on average was asked per pupil per month.

If you identify this pattern in your own classroom and wish to shift questioning more towards the pupils, hopefully the activities throughout this book will help to achieve that. It's also worth looking into what Professor Dillon calls the 'pedagogy of questioning', where teachers ask themselves generic questions to guide and structure their teaching –

What is it that pupils are to know or learn from this coming lesson?
To which questions does that knowledge or learning represent an answer?

Further questions arise from these –

What do I want the answer for?
What shall I do with the answer?

And subsequently –

How did the questions work?
Which next questions might work better?

Honing teacher-initiated questioning goes hand in hand with encouraging children to ask further questions that ideally become more relevant and probing as time goes by.

There are many ways of classifying questions – in pondering answers to those mentioned previously, you will already have identified a number of categories. We also think it's useful for children to have some insight into the sorts of questions they can ask and under what circumstances in order to both refine and increase the flexibility of their questioning skills.

For instance, in a now quite old study (1967), educator Douglas Barnes looked at question types as part of a larger project exploring the 'whole language environment' of a classroom. He found that among teacher-initiated questions, many were factual (what?) questions to elicit naming or information; reasoning (how? and why? questions) where pupils are invited to think aloud as they work their way towards possible answers; open questions that do not necessarily call for reasoning and where a number of possible answers would be acceptable; and 'control' or procedural questions to guide the behaviour the teacher wants from the children. Clearly, questions of a similar procedural type can come from the children – Can I go to the toilet? Shall we do this work in our best books? Can I sharpen my pencil? Steve keeps talking to me and I can't do my work. Will you tell him to stop, please?

(Ref: Language, the Learner and the School.)

Educationalists Nora Morgan and Juliana Saxton, in their book 'Asking Better Questions', go into rather more detail by identifying three broad categories; questions which elicit information, questions which shape understanding (those that help to connect the facts and elaborate how pupils are thinking and feeling about the material); questions that press for reflection and that invite the pupils to think both critically and creatively.

Within these broad categories, we find questions that call for a range of thinking skills of various levels of sophistication. Procedural questions from the teacher – questions that oil the wheels of a lesson – can involve the children and are of a higher level than the pupil-initiated procedural questions mentioned previously. Questions such as 'Do we have enough to go on?' 'Where might we find that information?' and 'What do you think would be the best order in which to do these things?' and

'Is there anything in the lesson so far that you don't understand?' invite the children to give some thought to them before answering.

Questions that focus on making connections embody one of the key elements of creative thinking (another being the ability to look at things in different ways, from different perspectives – a great activity for this is the well-known 'how many things can you use paperclips for?'). Other examples warranting deeper discussion include – How is the world different now to the Victorian era that we've just been studying? What effect do you think that increasingly sophisticated AI will have on our lives? What are the common features of the two short stories we've just read?

The shaping of children's understanding can also be accomplished by asking them to restate and more specifically define what is meant – skills that are also useful during discussions and philosophical enquiries, as we'll see later. . . What do you mean by 'hero'? Can you say that in another way that will help me to understand? What is it about the poem that you dislike so much? What would a poem need to have to make it more enjoyable or powerful for you?

The same broad category of questions that help to shape understanding incorporates questions that encourage the expression of opinions, attitudes, biases and points of view. These include the popular 'would you rather' kinds of questions that are often used as warmups prior to discussions and philosophical enquiries and can be great fun to try out – Would you rather be Batman or Spiderman? Would you rather be much better looking or much more intelligent? Would you rather travel back in time or forwards into the future? Would you rather have more time or more money? Extend the activity by asking children to think about and offer reasons for their decisions. Also, once children have chosen a would-you-rather option, ask them to think about the consequences if they really did have, say, spider powers or if they really could travel back through time.

Activity: Would You Rather

Many more examples can be found online, and of course children can be invited to make up their own. Some questions of this kind require children to ponder quite deeply, especially if the idea embodied in a question is new to them. A good source of such questions is to be found in biophysicist Gregory Stock's popular 'Kids' Book of Questions', which features some actual 'would you rather' questions or ones that can be created by rephrasing, such as; Would you rather your parents gave you more pocket money or spent more time with you? Would you rather be a great scientist or a great sport star (you can pick your science or sport)? Would you rather live to be 90 in good health or have enough money to do whatever you wanted?

The game can also focus on philosophical themes such as beauty, consciousness, time, mind, truth, etc. Invite the children to come up with questions based on these. Would you rather be more physically good looking or cleverer? Would you rather be able to know if people were telling the truth or have the ability to convince people that you were, even if you were lying?

Activity: Question Match

Show the children Figure 1.1 and ask them to match up the example questions with the categories that are listed. Take it further by asking for other examples in each category.

Task: Here is a list of question types and a list of questions.
Match the questions to the categories.

1) Questions that ask you to remember.
2) Questions that test your understanding.
3) Questions that ask you to solve a problem or work something out.
4) Questions that ask you to reason something through.
5) Questions that ask you to make a judgement.
6) Questions that ask you to have a new idea.

A) Can you rephrase the sentence, 'Toxic emissions are detrimental to the environment'?
B) What are the main reasons the author wrote the short story using dialogue only?
C) What did you have for lunch yesterday?
D) Do you think Marvel comic characters are better than DC comic characters, and why/why not?
E) Which is the odd one out in this list, and why? Bright, shining, brilliant, loud, luminous.
F) How do you think we could ease the problem of too much traffic on this country's roads?
G) What is a simile?
H) Would it be better if children were allowed to leave school at 16?
I) What is meant by the proverb 'All that glitters is not gold'?
J) Looking at the picture, how do we know it's been raining?

Figure 1.1 Matching a list of questions with their appropriate categories.

Some of Gregory Stock's questions touch on the same kind of moral dilemmas that are explored during philosophy sessions. So, for instance, 'A close friend tells you in confidence that (s)he's going to cheat in an upcoming test. What, if anything, do you do about it?' 'Would you rather have £100 to spend on yourself or £500 to spend on your family and/or friends?' 'If you could take a pill that could make you either stronger or braver, which would you choose and why?' Incidentally, Gregory Stock has also produced a more adult version of the book called simply, 'The Book of Questions.'

Activity: Strength of Reasons

That 'why' adds another dimension to the question and is linked to 'because', which encourages reasoning. One way of helping children with this is to explore the notion of the strength of the reasons. Begin by offering a situation in the form of a question, such as the one mentioned previously about the friend cheating. Then ask the class to come up with a range of responses (they don't have to be ones that the children themselves would actually do).

Now discuss which responses are positive, which are negative and which could be either, depending on your point of view. Next, offer the children a 1–6 scale, where one indicates any weak reasons and six more robust reasons. So – 'A close friend tells you in confidence that (s)he's going to cheat in an upcoming test. What, if anything, do you do about it?'

I wouldn't do anything because I don't want to lose that person as a friend. This could be regarded as a strong reason since the friendship is close. But is it a positive or a negative reason, given that the responder knows that cheating in tests is wrong?

I would advise my friend not to cheat because of the risk of getting caught. This might be seen as a positive and morally sound piece of advice and, in this case, you can add the 'what-if' pattern of thinking, so, 'What if your friend said (s)he was going to cheat anyway because getting low marks would mean being given a bad end-of-term report that would get the child into trouble with their parents?' Or, 'What if your friend offered you money not to tell about the cheating?' Or, 'What if your friend cheated, got great marks and received a certificate of excellence in assembly?' Would your reaction be different if, for whatever reason, you got low marks and received no praise?

Powers of reasoning can be elevated by asking questions that develop critical assessment and value judgements. In their book, Norah Morgan and Juliana Saxton use the example of the plaque that was carried aboard the robot space probe Pioneer 10, launched in 1972. The plaque was a depiction of a human male and female, that the probe came from the third planet orbiting the sun, together with information about where the solar system is located. Images of the plaque are readily available online. The probe's trajectory took it out of the solar system and into deep space. The purpose of the plaque was to 'introduce humankind' to any advanced alien races that might be out there exploring the universe (a dangerous move or not?).

In that context, Morgan and Saxton ask posit questions such as –

How could you change the plaque to make it say who we are as humans?

Do you think that at $150 million (at 1972 values, around $1,130,125,899 in 2024 according to CalculateMe.com), the Pioneer 10 project cost was justified?

Does it matter to you or not if there is advanced life in outer space? Why/why not?

Would you rather the money spent on space exploration went instead towards ending poverty around the world?

Morgan and Saxton emphasise that such categories are not hierarchical, even though the questions within them call for thinking skills of varying depth and sophistication, nor do they even suggest that theirs is the only way of categorising questions. So, for instance, we find questions that –

Elaborate and Redirect – Steve, can you add anything to Tony's list of reasons?

Evaluate – What are the things you like most about this school and why?

Call for Inference – What do you think you know about this character, and why?

Compare – What are the similarities and differences between X and Y?

Solve Problems – How might we best deal with the litter problem around the school?

Express Feelings – How do you feel about X? What is your reaction to Y?

Check Information/Ideas – Does that make sense? Do you have any other questions?

Then there are the familiar categories of closed and open questions, where closed questions close off options to a simple yes or no/true or false response, while open questions open up thinking to more possibilities

Establishing a Questioning Classroom 11

Figure 1.2 A visual of the main open question words of where, when, who, what, how and why.

through the big question words of where, when, what, who, how and why, as in Figure 1.2.

Activity: Questions Around the Star

Firstly, ask children to research the etymology of the big open-question words. Then, pick one of the words and invite the class to ask as many questions beginning with the word as they can in, say, two minutes. These can be recorded, and the ones that can't be answered may be researched afterwards. This can be seen as an extension of the activity 'Questions Around a Pencil' on page 3.

We can also identify rhetorical questions that are asked for effect rather than with the expectation of an answer (Do you realise it's your time you are wasting as well as mine? Ah, we remember it well!); leading questions that prompt or encourage a desired answer, for example, 'Did you realise

Ben wasn't wearing a school tie?' as opposed to the non-leading question, 'What was Ben wearing?' although here the desired response re the tie might form part of the answer. Some sources also include 'tag questions', where an interrogative is tagged on at the end of a sentence, as in, 'You're not wearing your school tie, are you?' Also, so-called choice questions, which we came across in the 'Would You Rather' activity. So, would you prefer chicken or fish? Do you think I should wear my white shirt or my blue one? And so on. Hypothetical questions are usually based on opinions rather than facts and often involve flights of fancy – If you could have one superpower, what would it be? If you could meet any character, real or fictional, who would that be and why?

Activity: Leading Questions

Here's a list of questions that lead or draw children towards a certain response. Ask the class to restate them as non-leading questions. Firstly though, invite the children to consider why these are leading questions in the first place.

What's wrong with that idea? (The assumption is that something is indeed wrong with the idea.)

Did you find the story went on too long? (Implying that the opinion here is that the story was too long.)

Can you see the problem with this argument? (I.e. there is a problem with the argument.)

How many other ways can you think of to solve this problem? (Suggesting that there is more than one way to solve the problem.)

How bored were you by this poem? (Implying that a degree of boredom was inevitable.)

What did you find difficult about that exercise? (Suggesting that the exercise was difficult.)

Should different people be treated differently? (Repetition of the word emphasises difference.)

You were in town on Saturday, weren't you? (The interrogative implies that this person was in town on Saturday, and the questioner knows this.)

How carefully were you paying attention when you bumped into one another? (Suggesting that they weren't paying attention.)

Would you rather work on this older tablet or that newer and faster one? (Leading the responder to prefer the newer and faster tablet.)

Questions can also be categorised according to the kinds of thinking they encourage or require –

Questions that draw upon prior knowledge call for recognising, recollecting, identifying and defining.

Questions that test comprehension/understanding or require rephrasing, explaining, defining, describing, comparing and associating.

Questions aimed at solving problems require classifying, reasoning, selecting, applying and hypothesising.

Questions that call for reasoning are answered through analysing, sifting evidence, discriminating, inferring and ranking.

Questions calling for creativity require combining, perceiving flexibly, improving, developing – all underpinned by playfulness and the recognition that to have the best ideas we need to generate lots of ideas.

Questions that call for evaluation, incorporate summarising, assessing, arguing, judging, selecting and prioritising as well as reasoning.

Another technique when enquiring is called the three-step approach and might apply to most or all of the question types mentioned previously and their associated thinking skills –

What do we know?

What do we think we know?

What can we ask or do to find out more?

Activity: Categorising Questions

Give the class a list of questions and ask the children if they can state what kinds of questions they are. Answers need not refer to the 'formal' or standard categories mentioned previously; indeed, there's a certain value in children creating their own classifications, which can lead to some useful discussions around the notion of knowledge and, as Postman and Weingartner say, 'what's worth knowing?' So the question about how many pencils there are in the world right now could be classed as one that has a definite (though ever-changing) right answer but one that can never be known. However, children who decide that it's a silly, pointless or boring question are certainly entitled to their opinions and open the doorway to the notion of relevance.

Here's a suggested selection of questions to try out on the class –

1. What is 2+2?
2. What is the capital city of England?

3. Do you like orange juice?
4. Are you tall?
5. What is green?
6. What is your favourite film?
7. How far away are the stars?
8. Why do we need to have best friends?
9. How can someone find true happiness?

Each of these questions can act as stepping-stones to further discussions and questions.

What is 2+2 can form the basis for asking whether numbers are human inventions or are actually 'built into' nature, i.e. were they invented or discovered? (See Brian Clegg's 'Are Numbers Real?' in the Bibliography.) Question two about the capital of England can generate a spray of further questions, such as those on page 1. Example three raises questions about what it means to 'like' something and whether different kinds of 'liking' apply to different things: orange juice, a book, a friend and so on. Some children will express 'it depends' or contingent thinking in response to question four: it depends on what you mean by tall, or tall in comparison with what or whom? With regard to question five, perceptive children will recognise its ambiguity – do you mean what are the names of some things that are coloured green, or what is 'greenness', or do you mean green in the sense of naiveté or inexperience? Question six can prompt reflection on why we have favourite things, with the realisation that they are our favourites for a whole raft of reasons. Question seven can also encourage contingent thinking, although some children might point out the weakness of the question since stars are scattered throughout the universe at an infinite range of distances. Question eight might trigger a host of subjective responses, as well as reflecting on what 'best' means in this context. Question nine is similar in that children can be invited to define 'happiness' as well as probe into the meaning of 'true', and whether it's possible to have 'untrue' or false happiness and whether that's the same as pretending to be happy.

Children will implicitly come to realise that –

Different kinds of questions prompt different sorts of responses.
Questions are useful even if there isn't one clear-cut answer.
Many questions act as stepping-stones to further questions.
Suppositions, opinions and judgements are sometimes perfectly acceptable answers, especially when supported by reasons.
Questions can be precisely worded or ambiguous and 'fuzzy', each kind being useful in different ways.

Establishing a Questioning Classroom 15

| Activity: Exemplar Questions |

You can run this game before or after discussing some of the different kinds of questions with the children. Offer these categories and invite the children to find some examples of each –
Questions lead to answers that are always right for everybody. For instance, what is the highest mountain in the world?
Questions whose answers are different now from what they used to be. For instance, what is the outermost planet in the solar system? It used to be Pluto, but in 2006 the International Astronomical Union downgraded it to a 'dwarf planet', making Neptune the outermost true planet in the solar system (although what might we mean by 'true' here?). This also touches on the point that facts are provisional. It used to be a fact that Pluto was a planet, but now it's a fact that it isn't. See also the etymology of 'fact' on page 2.
Questions where different people's opinions can all be counted as 'right' answers, such as 'What is your favourite food?' It would also be interesting to ask the children to define 'right' more precisely and by thinking of some synonyms.
Questions whose answer nobody knows for sure, such as 'Are there other universes?' (Note that in his book 'Parallel Universes: the search for other worlds', American theoretical physicist Fred Alan Wolf asserts that the fact that quantum physics 'works' virtually guarantees that other universes exist.)

| Activity: Questions Around Concepts |

This is about generating questions based on bare facts or ideas. Ask children what questions they can think of around –

Mount Everest
Onomatopoeia
Twelve
String

This is similar to the technique of asking, 'This is the answer – what are the questions?' Take the activity further by asking children to think of further words/facts/ideas and then come up with questions about them.

A Question of Relevance

This topic is thoroughly explored by Postman and Weingartner in their book 'Teaching as a Subversive Activity', where they vociferously argue that current educational models (at least in the U.S.) are largely irrelevant for most students insofar as the curriculum does not address issues and problems that concern learners directly, but instead consists of bodies of knowledge that are 'delivered' and then examined – what educationalist John Abbott calls the 'tell 'em and test 'em' curriculum.

It's not our intention to debate the issue here, and indeed, if a child is willing or even happy to study hard within the given curriculum because she has a certain career in mind and needs to get good grades, who are we to argue with that? What we will say though, and feel strongly about, is that cultivating a questioning attitude in children, together with the attendant thinking skills that this engenders, is relevant *per se* as far as their ability to learn is concerned, not just during their school years but beyond in life generally.

In their chapter on 'What's Worth Knowing?' Postman and Weingartner probe more deeply into the issue of relevance by offering a list of questions that they feel many students would find apposite in their lives. These include –

- How do you want to be similar to or different from adults you know when *you* become an adult?
- What, if anything, seems to be worth dying for? How did you come to believe this?
- What kind of person would you most like to be?
- How can you tell a good person from a bad person?
- What do you think are some of humanity's most important ideas, and why do you think this?

Also, explore the question in terms of 'good' ideas, such as discoveries in medicine, with 'bad' ideas, such as the development of the atom bomb (although it hastened the end of the Second World War, so does that make it a 'good' idea?)

The authors go on to offer questions that teachers can ask themselves to encourage students' curiosity and their own ability to ask questions, among which are –

- Will your questions increase students' desire to learn as well as their capacity to learn?
- Will your questions cultivate a greater love of learning? And is a desire to learn the same as a love of learning?
- Will your questions develop students' confidence to learn?
- In order to generate answers, will your questions prompt further enquiry in the students?
- Will your questions help students to live more effectively in society?

Although we heartily support Postman and Weingartner's ethos, it's hardly likely that our educational system will change along the lines they suggest, perhaps not even in the long term. However, we feel it's worth taking a little time to ponder the questions posed earlier so that we may refine our ability to ask questions that are not only relevant to the children's learning within the curriculum as it stands but also those that help them to become more effective learners throughout life.

Effective Learners

Postman and Weingartner offer advice as to what effective and enthusiastic learners 'look like'. They –

Have learned how to ask meaningful questions.
Examine and are happy to alter their assumptions.
Are cautious in making generalisations.
Are keen to verify what they believe.
Are careful and thorough observers.
Are not afraid of being wrong and are prepared to change their beliefs as necessary.
Tend to gather information and reflect on it before giving answers or making judgements.
Are flexible in their thinking and in coming up with strategies for solving problems.
Have a high regard for facts, while realising that many facts are provisional and can change. To demonstrate this, have children look through old science books, pick out some facts and check with more recent sources to see if the facts are still accurate.
Realise that language controls perceptions – for more on this try www.gofluent.com/us-en/blog/how-language-affects-the-way-we-think/
Don't feel the need always to have final, clear-cut answers. They are not fearful of saying 'I don't know' and can tolerate ambiguity and uncertainty, realising too that some questions may not have solutions and perhaps never will.

Bloom's Taxonomy of Thinking

American educationalist Benjamin Bloom created a model for classifying ways of thinking that underpinned many of the developments of the curriculum in the 1960s and 70s. However, authors Mel Rockett and Simon Percival, in their book 'Thinking for Learning', point out that Bloom's taxonomy has at times been misinterpreted based on the assumption that younger pupils or those that are termed 'less able' are only capable of dealing with the lower 'rungs' of Bloom's thinking ladder. Thinking, though, is more complex than this and does not develop in the strict hierarchical way that the taxonomy might suggest. . .

On a personal note, at the last school where Steve worked, we had an activities week that took place towards the end of the summer term. During this time, the normal curriculum was set aside and staff were invited to offer a different course that pupils could choose to attend. One time, a group of Year Nine pupils asked if Steve would run a fighting fantasy war gaming week. He said that he'd like to but didn't understand the rules of the game. The pupils sighed tolerantly and said it didn't matter because *they* understood the rules.

So the course went ahead. On Monday morning the participants turned up early and rearranged the classroom furniture to suit themselves. Some of the pupils chose to paint the small metal figures used in war gaming scenarios, while other groups immediately started up a campaign. Steve had brought a stack of books to read since he was surplus to requirements, but at one point became distracted when he noticed one group in particular. It consisted of about half a dozen Year Nine boys and one Year Seven boy, who seemed to be in charge. Steve happened to know that this boy was in the lowest set for all of his school subjects and was routinely labelled as 'less able', yet here he was, leading the older children in the campaign. Intrigued, he went over and asked if he was, indeed, the 'games master'. The boy was painfully shy and just nodded. Steve asked the rest of the group why he had been chosen and was told 'because he understands the rules better than we do.' When asked what that meant, one of the Year Nines delved into his Adidas sports bag and pulled out a Warhammer battle manual. When Steve glanced through it, he saw that the language was adult-level and the rules for running a campaign were, indeed, very complicated. It turned out that this young boy had not only read the entire manual but had comprehended it *and memorised it*. Not only that, but as the games master he was able to make reasoned decisions, deal with dissent and arbitrate when disagreements occurred, calm any players who started to lose their temper and clarify any issues the players had with any of the rules. His abilities within the context of the game were truly spectacular, and yet they never showed themselves in any ordinary lessons.

Steve was so impressed by the boy's talents that he went to the Games Workshop in town and asked if he could buy one of the manuals. He was, by this time, teaching part-time and doing some CPD work in other schools. He wanted to tell teachers this anecdote to point out the danger of misjudging some pupils by making assumptions about what they were capable of. The assistant at the shop told him that the manual was part of the basic gaming pack that also included paints and some metal figures. When Steve said that he only wanted the manual, the manager was called and Steve told him the story. He reacted quite emotionally and asked Steve to wait a few minutes. Steve heard him rummaging about in the stockroom upstairs and he came back down with a well-thumbed copy of the manual, which he gave to Steve for free, 'Because', he said 'I was exactly like the young boy in your story, and if I didn't have my passion for fighting fantasy games I would never have had the confidence to go for an interview to be manager of this shop.'

Steve will never forget the young boy (and often wonders what became of him) because he taught him a salutary lesson about pupils' hidden abilities and how these can so easily be overlooked. And he still has the battle manual, though even now he doesn't fully understand the rules!

The story also highlights Rockett's and Percival's point that Bloom's taxonomy is not a ladder that children climb, more or less successfully: the ability to think in a sophisticated way, with other attendant attributes, is strongly influenced by a child's motivation and the context within which thinking is required to take place. We suspect that the Year Seven boy in the story would be able to deal with difficult problems in Maths, for instance, if they were somehow related to fighting fantasy games!

Simply put, Bloom's taxonomy begins with 'simple thinking' and little understanding, to use Rockett's and Percival's phrasing, to advanced thinking and full understanding – though one might wonder what 'full' understanding could mean. The stages of thinking in between are –

Knowledge – Mainly taking the form of something previously learned.
Comprehension – The ability to express ideas in one's own words.
Application – Being able to use knowledge or skill in a new situation.
Analysis – Understanding the relationship between ideas and the ability to explore and question them.
Evaluation – The ability to use criteria to judge ideas or situations.
Synthesis – Connecting concepts to form new ideas or insights: the ability to create.

The relevance of our exploration of questioning skills is that, as teachers, we can put questions to the children within any and all of the 'stages' of thinking outlined by Bloom. We can also be more aware of the kinds of thinking that underpin the questions that pupils ask. As an aid to this, it's possible to add some detail to each of Bloom's thinking categories, as in Figure 1.3.

In this case, the example questions focus on a story the pupils have read, but the same categories and the questions they generate can apply to any subject or topic area –

Bloom's Taxonomy.

Knowledge related thinking:	**Example questions:**
Telling	What do you remember about the story we read?
Listing	
Finding	What characters appear in the story?
	Where does the hero first appear?
Comprehension related thinking:	How would you sum up the story in your own words?
Restating/summarising	Are there other stories that are similar? If so, how?
Exemplifying	
Concluding	Do you think this is a good story? Why/why not?
Application related thinking:	What have you learned from this story that you could use in your own writing?
Modelling	
Demonstrating	How would you present what you've learned to your classmates?
Analysis related thinking:	What kind of story would you call this, and how do you know?
Classifying	
Comparing and contrasting	What similarities and differences do you notice with other stories of this kind?
Evaluation related thinking:	How highly do you rate this story and why?
Critiquing/judging	What are the story's particular strengths? And do you notice any weakness in the writing?
Synthesis related thinking:	Using the elements and motifs in the story, can you now create a storyline for one of your own?
Creating	
Imagining	If the story you've read or your own had a sequel, what would be the plot?

Figure 1.3 A suggested hierarchy of thinking skills devised by educator and psychologist Benjamin Bloom.

Activity: Questions Around a Story

Show the class the following short story. Either ask children questions about it (some examples follow the story and/or use some from Figure 1.3) or invite them to come up with questions of their own that reflect different kinds of thinking as outlined by Bloom.

The Box With the Answer

All of the children knew that Ben Lee was a wizard, although most of the adults in the town – unless their hearts were young – believed that he was just a simple shopkeeper. His little store, *Ben Lee's Jokes & Tricks*, sat tucked away in a small yard just off the High Street. It had been there for years, longer in fact than anyone could remember.

Everybody knew about that shop, and it clearly made a profit, but it never seemed crowded. And if by chance a child came in just to get away from things, just to be in a quiet place where he would not be troubled, strangely no other customers entered. Yet if that young boy was thinking of his friends, quite wonderfully, oddly, coincidentally, the bell above the door would tinkle, the boy would turn and there would be Jamie or Jo, Sarah or Ian – his best friends merely passing by, who had decided on a whim to drop in.

And that was Ben Lee's wizardry, the kind that goes on peacefully behind the busy surfaces of things. It was not the sort of magic that was all bangs and flashes, fizzles and flying through the air. No, it was like still waters, deep and mysterious, that ripple when a pebble is tossed in.

On this particular day, a Saturday, quite a number of children thought about Ben Lee's joke shop and decided to pay it a visit. Certain children that is, the ones who needed to be there. Within a few minutes of each other, young Dean Blencoe turned up and one of the evil Henderson brothers (not Stonehead, the worse of the two, but Flicknose, who was three years younger); and Katie Day and John Doe and a few more, so that the shop seemed busier than it had been for some time.

For a little while, all of the children browsed among the shelves and spinners, the wallboards and display stands as though they had come to buy tricks. Then Dean Blencoe frowned and scratched his head and thought to himself, "Why am I here?"

On sensing that by some mysterious means, Ben Lee clapped his hands to capture the children's attention. He was a short, rather round and very jolly figure wearing a bright blue waistcoat and braces with a red bow tie that looked as though it would start to spin like an aeroplane propeller at any second.

"Young friends, thank you for coming along. I'd like to take this opportunity to show you something that the man in the white van has only just delivered." He reached beneath the counter and brought out a somewhat battered grey cardboard box, a bit like a shoebox that had been kicked around by the shoes it once contained.

"This," said Ben Lee with a sense of great occasion, "is the Box with the Answer!"

"The answer to what?" asked Katie Day with the rather petulant tone in her voice that had been growing there for the last two years.

"To the question you ask, of course." Ben Lee was not a bit put out by the way Katie screwed up her face and drilled her finger against her temple, suggesting he was mad. "You may all think of one question and then take a peek inside. Who'd like to go first?"

"Me!" said Henderson in his big and blustering way. He pushed through the small gathering of children and shouldered his way to the front. Everyone else grumbled and muttered at his behaviour, but Ben Lee only smiled and lifted the lid of the box just enough for Stonehead to slide his hand through.

"What is your question, Neville?" Ben Lee asked, using Stonehead's true name, that he tried to keep secret from the world.

"How can I get rich?"

"Hmm, an interesting question. Remove what's in the box to find the answer."

"What the – what?" Neville cried in bemusement, opening his hand to look at the egg he'd brought out. "What use is this to me?" And he flung it hard down onto the countertop – where it came to rest gently without a single crack in the shell.

"Next!" said Ben Lee, offering the box.

"Me!" Katie Day took her turn. "How can I be the happiest person in the whole world?" Putting on her self-important and giggling face, she delved into the box and pulled out – an egg. Perhaps it was the same egg that Neville Henderson had found because that one now was nowhere to be seen.

"That's just stupid!" she declared as she made to dash the egg against the wall then thought better of it and placed it carefully on the counter.

John Doe went next, wanting to know how he could be top of the class. Then Dean Blencoe took his turn, asking what was the capital of Peru. Actually, he knew the answer to that, but he pulled an egg from the box anyway, although he found the shell impossible to crack. In fact, all of the children drew out what appeared to be the self-same egg.

Until it came to Dale's turn. When Ben Lee offered him the box, the boy shrugged and looked a bit self-conscious.

"Are you all right, Dale?" Ben Lee wondered in concern.

"I'm OK. I was going to ask what the future holds and what I'd make of my life. But I think I'm happy just to wait and see thank you anyway."

The rest of the children muttered unkind names for him under their breath, but not too loudly because they knew he'd only pull out an egg like they had all done. Dale shrugged again and looked sheepish, but he stuck his hands in his pockets to show that he was determined in his choice.

Ben Lee smiled at him as kindly as he had at Neville. "Very well," he said, "that is your choice. And now –" He became brisk and businesslike – "I am about to close up my shop for tonight. But because you've all been such good sports, you may select any joke, trick, prop or disguise from my shelves and take it away completely free of charge!"

There was a short bout of cheering from the children and in great excitement they made their selections. Neville Henderson, without knowing quite why, picked a pack of cards that always turned up a Royal Flush no matter which cards he tried to select. Katie Day settled on a grumpy-looking mask that slid off her face no matter how securely she tried to fix it on. For some reason the whole rigmarole made her laugh. John Doe found himself taking a book of puzzles and riddles, and Dean Blencoe picked up a dice on which all of the faces showed a six.

And Dale Featherstone – though he thought this very odd later on – simply waved to Ben Lee, opened the door of the shop and went out into the big, wide, busy world.

And soon, the shop was empty, save for Ben Lee himself. He didn't bother to tidy up because the shop would do that for itself through the night. But he did put the Box that has the Answer back under the counter and, just before he left, he cracked open the egg and saw that it was full of time and space, stars and wonderful dreams.

*

What are the names of some of the characters in the story? (knowledge, recall)

What genre does the story fit into? (comprehension, comparing, analysis, classifying)

What could the egg symbolise? (You might ask children to find out what a symbol is first.) (researching)

What writing techniques has the writer used that you might use in your own stories? (application, modelling)

Do you think this is a good story? Explain why or why not. (evaluation, critiquing, judging)

Could you write another story of the same kind, where Mr Lee uses some other kind of magic or a story that focuses on one or more of the children after they have left the shop with their gift? (synthesis, imagining, creating)

Take it further by asking children to wonder what question they would ask the box that has the answer and the reason for their choice.

Activity: Bloom's Taxonomy Around a Topic

Choose a topic that you have studied with the class. Show the children Bloom's taxonomy and invite them to come up with questions about the topic that they think fit into the different categories.

Problems With Questioning

In the Introduction, we looked briefly at factors that might inhibit taking time to ask and answer questions. From a teacher's point of view, curriculum pressure might be the most significant issue. Inviting children's questions allows a topic to be explored more thoroughly but takes up lesson time. From the pupils' point of view, some children might be fearful of asking a question that could be regarded as silly or that shows up their apparent ignorance. Further, using whole-class questioning as a pedagogical technique means that, while plenty of hands might go up, only one pupil can respond each time unless other children have the knowledge to expand on the answer, or suggest a different answer. Some pupils who are rarely picked to give an answer might get fed up with trying and slip into 'passive mode'. Other children, who don't want to answer questions for whatever reason, might try a number of avoidance techniques such as not making eye contact with the teacher, pretending to think about the question while other hands go up, or putting up a hand when the child knows the teacher makes a point of asking those pupils with hands down.

Other issues include some pupils who try to dominate the process by vigorously putting a hand up and even calling out; the teacher asking too many questions at the expense of other teaching techniques; introducing difficult questions prematurely and favouring some pupils over others.

Benefits of Questioning

That said, most if not all teachers will judge that the benefits of devoting some lesson time to questioning outweigh the disadvantages. Questioning from teacher and pupils –

Aids recollection of previously taught ideas and facts.
Helps to connect prior knowledge, thus deepening understanding and creating possible further insights.
Serves as feedback for any difficulties or misunderstandings some children might have with the material.
Creates opportunities for pupils who struggle with writing to show their understanding orally.
Serves as a means of introducing and practising the different kinds of thinking outlined in Bloom's taxonomy.

Activities to Encourage Pupil Questioning

Brainstorming. Set the class a problem or an issue to talk about and invite the children to think 'on the hoof', i.e. letting ideas pop into mind without thinking too deeply and without evaluating ideas at that stage. In other words, utilising the creative principle of 'to have our best ideas, we need to have lots of ideas.' Brainstorming can be a whole-class activity, or children can be put into groups. Usually a time limit is set, after which ideas are shared and pupils have the opportunity to ask questions about them. It's important to emphasise that all ideas and suggestions are acceptable, even if subsequently some of them are discarded (at least for now. Discarded ideas might become relevant in another context, and as writers one of our maxims is that no idea is ever wasted).

Another way of 'harvesting' ideas is to pose a problem or issue, split the class into small groups and ask the groups to discuss and list their ideas. Subsequently, bring the class together again for a sharing session. To get this activity going, you might look at what we have to say about the 'Ambiguous Shapes Grid' on page 33 and how it can be used to brainstorm possible solutions to a problem.

Turning statements into questions. Present the class with a number of statements and ask children to turn them into open questions. Having a poster of the 'Question Star' (page 11) with the main open-question words, where, when, why, etc., on display allows children to frame their questions more effectively. Take the activity further by showing children how to 'trim' open questions by imposing a time limit for discussion, setting a word limit for answers or limit the number of ideas/reasons/ answers you want the children to give. This is good training for keeping to the point in philosophical enquiries. So instead of the question 'What is happiness?' you can trim it by asking, 'Can you think of four situations that help to define or explore happiness?' or, 'Explore the concept of happiness – do as much as you can in ten minutes?'

Use pictures as a stimulus for framing questions. Although we'll look at this again later, the process is also thoroughly explored in our 'Visualising Literacy and How to Teach It'.

Clarity of Language

One aspect of developing children's questioning skills is to make them aware of the importance of framing questions using clear and precise language, which helps to avoid ambiguity and uncertainty. One effective way of doing this is to teach children contingent ('it depends') thinking, a natural method for making this familiar being the philosophical enquiry, which we'll explore later. Another technique is to restate an idea using different words, perhaps by saying, 'So am I right in thinking that what you mean is . . . ?'

For example, in one book we read as part of our research, the author posed the question, 'If you didn't exist, would you be missed?' This immediately raised further questions in our minds. Does the question mean if I suddenly ceased to exist or if I had never existed? And in what sense is 'missed' being used? My local pub landlord might miss me in one sense when I stopped visiting for a pie and a pint. My wife would miss me in quite another way (I hope).

Although our initial judgement was that the question was unclear, the fact that it raised further questions is also a positive.

Activity: Ambiguous Words

Present the class with a list of words that can have two or more meanings and ask children a) to tease out these meanings and b) to use each meaning in a question sentence. One example is the word 'miss.' Questions that show different meanings for the word might be –

- Did you miss the bus yesterday?
- Will you miss me when I'm away?
- Does Miss Bowman still live next door to you?
- Do you agree with the proverb that 'A miss is as good as a mile'?

Another example is 'run' –

- Have you heard that he's going to run for president?
- Do you think you can run faster than me?
- Have you noticed that Miss has a run in her tights?
- I see that Tony is having a run of good luck.
- What time is the next train on the London to Sheffield run?
- How many runs did you score in the cricket match on Saturday?

Incidentally, the Reader's Digest website claims that 'run' has the most meanings of any word in the English language – 645 of them! (www.rd.com/article/most-complicated-word-in-english/)

Activity: Reflective Questioning on Learning

As children become more familiar with different kinds of questions and feel more comfortable and confident about asking them, you can present them with questions that invite them to reflect on their own learning. And while they might not wish to share some or even any of their answers, when they do this, it can provide useful feedback for you in refining your own pedagogy.

The kind of questions we're thinking of include –

What do you think were the most important ideas in today's lesson?
What facts or ideas did you find most interesting?

Were the most interesting facts/ideas also the most important ones? And what do you think the word 'important' means here?

Did you feel confused or puzzled by any of the ideas in the lesson? What were they? Do you have the confidence to ask for further explanations?

What is the best way for you to learn? For example, by listening to explanations, reading about them, discussing ideas with classmates, writing out ideas in your own words, looking at diagrams, more than one of these or some other method?

Talk with your friends. How do they learn best?

How do you know that you understand something?

Is understanding the same as knowing?

As children become more experienced and confident in the questioning classroom, they are more likely to give reasons and supply evidence to back up their answers. So if you ask, 'How do you know that you understand something?' children might come back with; Because I can explain it in a different way/in my own words; I can connect it with things in the topic I learnt before; I can think of more questions to ask about it than I could come up with before.

This is a world away from 'I just do'. In the same way that a lack of training in thinking skills can leave people gullible and therefore vulnerable, so an evolving capacity to think critically provides a kind of mental and emotional shield that, ideally, takes the form of open-minded scepticism, which leads to probing questioning of the information in question (as it were).

Activity: Picture Exploration

An effective way of sharpening children's critical thinking skills is to make the thinking explicit; that is, to feed back to children the process of the thinking they've just done to supply you with an answer. We've touched on this notion in some previous books. In 'Visualising Literacy and How to Teach It', we explain a workshop technique where we use a black-and-white image of a frightened or angry-looking cat on a street corner. There's a strange comet-like light in the sky.

We begin by asking the children to 'be nosy', to notice something in the picture and tell us about it. It's as simple as that at first. So a child might say, 'I can see a cat.' And our reply is, 'Good, you noticed that cat. That's exactly what we've asked you to do.'

However, this simple notice-and-tell activity throws up other kinds of thinking. A child might say, 'Well, I think it's been raining.' So we ask for the reasoning behind that observation – 'What clues did you notice to give you that idea?' 'Well, I first noticed the puddles on the pavement, but then I saw that the sky looked all cloudy and the cat's fur is sticking up, maybe because it got wet in the rain.' So we reply, 'Well done, you noticed something that gave you the idea that it's been raining, but then sensibly you looked for other clues to make your idea stronger.' An observation based on evidence followed by an informed search for further evidence amounts to the inferential thinking that lies at the heart of the scientific method.

Another child might say, 'Well, I think the light in the sky is a firework, and that's what's making the cat look frightened.' Reply: 'Good, you've suggested a strong connection between two details in the picture.' A different child might say, 'Well, I think it's a comet.' This is an opportunity to do some speculative thinking – 'It's not really clear what the object is, so we can say maybe it's a firework, maybe it's a comet, or . . . ?' And invite further 'maybes'. You might also go back to the idea that it's reasonable to suppose that a firework might frighten the cat, but could there be other things that would frighten it; a passing car or another vehicle, someone shouting, the sight of another cat out of frame across the road, etc.

When we want children to do 'maybe thinking', we hold out a hand palm upwards. As children come up with ideas, we mark them off on our fingers. Then we explain that this technique helps us to do speculative thinking: imagine that the focus of our thinking – what we've noticed – is in the palm of the hand, while possible explanations radiate away from it along the fingers and thumb. Sometimes, children come up with so many maybes that we need to use both hands and, occasionally, have to borrow some from the children!

Although these are simple techniques, they are underpinned by important principles. The maybe-hand technique encourages multiple possibilities, a point reinforced by Postman and Weingartner, who emphasise 'the power of pluralising', where students are encouraged to offer not a reason, but reasons; not the cause, but the causes; not the meaning, but the meanings. Again, this imperative is an important element in scientific enquiry, but also in other areas of human endeavour.

During the picture game, a child might say, 'Well, I think that's an ugly cat.' One of us will respond by clasping our hands together and holding them like that, saying nothing for several seconds. This usually focuses the class's attention as the children wonder what Steve or Tony is doing. Then we slowly unclasp the hands and say, 'You did an interesting piece of thinking there. You noticed the cat, well done (raising one hand), and you gave me your opinion about it (raising the other hand). Sometimes, when we have opinions or make judgements, it's like keeping our hands locked together. By separating what we've noticed from our opinion about it, we can then take time to think more about that opinion – at least to wonder why we formed it.'

It's easy enough to make 'snap' judgements that can form within a second. If we lack the awareness to notice what we've done, and then to separate out the observation from the opinion, the 'obserpinion' as we've called it can harden and act as a nucleus for further observations that supposedly confirm the initial observation. This can lead to so-called confirmation bias and, ultimately, to rigid and dogmatic views and the tendency to prejudge, sometimes tangled up with an 'ism'; racism, sexism, ageism, etc.

Again, quoting Postman and Weingartner: they urge us to teach children to doubt, question and challenge. Such an attitude can express itself outwardly but is also a powerful tool for exploring and understanding oneself more deeply.

Questioning as a Subversive Activity

The entire content of Postman and Weingartner's book revolves around the notion of subverting the old 'factory' model of education, based as it is on the delivery of facts and their passive acceptance by students. However, a much more finely nuanced point is the possibility that pupil questioning can become subversive in the sense of challenging the notion that a teacher or adults generally are the repositories of knowledge, 'right answers' and truth. (Light travels in straight lines – page 1). Also, as children become more confident and incisive questioners, adults may feel uneasy if they don't know the answers, perhaps increasingly so if this happens too often. The strategy of 'I don't know, but how can we find out?' is useful here, together with the rationale that adults are still learning too. This highlights the point that learning can and should be a lifelong journey. Another move is to encourage children to research their own questions – more easily done these days with access to the Internet, with adult guidance and supervision – and share what they find with the class.

Teacher unease at not knowing the answer is a real phenomenon. The last time Steve witnessed it was during a workshop session with a Year Five class. It so happened that an Ofsted team was in the school and one of the inspectors was sitting in on his workshop. This didn't bother Steve because he wasn't 'in the system', but the young class teacher was and he was very nervous. He'd written out what he wanted to say on prompt cards, which trembled in his hands as he referred to them.

About ten minutes before the end of the lesson, he stopped Steve and said that we had to do the plenary now. Immediately, one of the children asked him what a plenary was. Steve had to admit that he didn't know where the word itself came from, but he understood that plenaries happened towards the end of a lesson, to sum up what had been going on.

(He checked afterwards, and it comes from late-Latin *plenarius*, meaning 'complete'.) Part of the teacher's plenary was to prompt the class to ask Steve any questions about his writing. He said, 'Ask Steve about the kinds of things that inspired him as a writer, perhaps his childhood.' One of the children immediately came back with, 'So Steve, what inspired you to be a writer? Your childhood, perhaps?' The inspector and Steve grinned at one another. To this day, he doesn't know if the child was being subversive or not!

In summary, developing children's questioning skills boosts their sense of ownership in the learning they do, which in turn strengthens their confidence and sense of self-esteem. They come to realise that asking questions doesn't flag up their ignorance but serves to highlight their curiosity and, more subtly, that we live in a world that is wonderful and mysterious in so many ways (see the wireless anecdote on page 4). Questioning cultivates a child's sense of wonder, not just of the natural world but of the creativity and ingenuity of the human race. This attitude of wonderment leads naturally to wanting to ponder the deeper questions, the deeper mysteries, of life.

Perhaps most importantly, as American educator and author John Holt has said, we know that education works when children are happy, energetic and involved.

2 Questioning and Creativity

Aspects of Creativity Include

A good sense of humour.
Playfulness that can take many forms.
Tolerance of others' ideas.
A healthy resilience to setbacks (which may be seen as further opportunities for learning).
Independence of judgement.
Feeling comfortable with ambiguity and uncertainty.
Raised self-esteem (helped by the pleasure of having ideas and in a learning environment that values them).

The realisation that the human mind is a wonderful thing: that we are capable of thinking in a variety of ways is uplifting. A useful metaphor is to consider the mind as a toolbox of thinking instruments and that effective thinking comes by choosing the right tool(s) for the job. (That said, we've come across some commentators who disapprove of the tools metaphor as being too 'mechanical' and simplistic. What do you think?)

Activity: Similes and Metaphors

Spend a little time offering the class other metaphors or similes for the mind, such as the mind is like a rocket because? The mind is a river because? The mind is a spider web because? Take the activity further by inviting children to come up with other metaphors of their own.

You can see that the 'creative attitude' overlaps with the questioning attitude. Indeed, since creativity arises out of noticing and questioning, we can argue that they are more or less the same thing. Creativity is also characterised by making connections to form new ideas and insights and the willingness to look at things in many ways.

DOI: 10.4324/9781003608714-2

Activity: Ambiguous Shapes

To both check on and further develop children's creativity, show them an ambiguous shape such as in Figure 2.1.

Say, 'What could it be? What does it remind you of?' and give the children a minute or so to come up with ideas. Responses we've had include –

Looking down on a tree that has had an X painted on the leaves.
A tree with a sticking plaster on it.
An expanding cloud of dust after a heavy metal X was dropped on the ground.
An X-shaped UFO resting on a cloud.
Looking down on a flower. The X represents the stamens.
Looking up through a sheet of glass at a curvy-shaped table. The X is the four-legged table stand.
Liquid spilt on an oblong table top, lapping around an X-shaped ornament.
A fried egg with a burst yolk that oddly looks like an X.
The Angel of the North on top of the hill.
Looking down on a drone flying over a large pond in a rectangular field.
A symbol for creativity – a cloud of ideas that, when they first appear, are not judged as wrong.

You can take the activity further by saying to the class, 'If this shape said something about a character, what do we learn?' Responses include –

Someone who's woolly-minded and often gets things wrong.
Someone who gets cross easily and likes to blow off steam.
Someone who likes to turn the tables on his enemies (that thought coming out of the table example in the previous list).

Figure 2.1 This visual encourages children to interpret an abstract and ambiguous shape.

A variation of the game is to take away the X and replace it with a different shape or to add colour. This is likely to produce another raft of ideas.

It's important to emphasise that the children shouldn't try too hard to have ideas since conscious mental effort will tend to slow or even seize up the process. The subconscious part of the mind is the seat of our creativity, such that once the task is specified, ideas will pop up 'out of the blue'. We also want to say something about originality. While an idea or question may be commonplace to us, a child might have had that idea for the first time, so it is original to her and should be respected as such.

> **Activity: Ambiguous Shapes Grid**

A more challenging game is to use a grid of ambiguous shapes, as in Figure 2.2, to suggest solutions to problems.

But before launching into this, ask the children to pick two or more shapes that have something in common; for instance, some of them feature squares, some have shapes within shapes, a couple are spirals and two of them (3/2 and 4/2) feature letters of the alphabet. This is a quick and easy way of boosting observational skills. Find a shape by counting underneath the bottom row and then up the selected column: 'along the corridor and up the stairs'.

For the next stage, either think of some problems yourself or ask the children to come up with suggestions. The problems might concern the

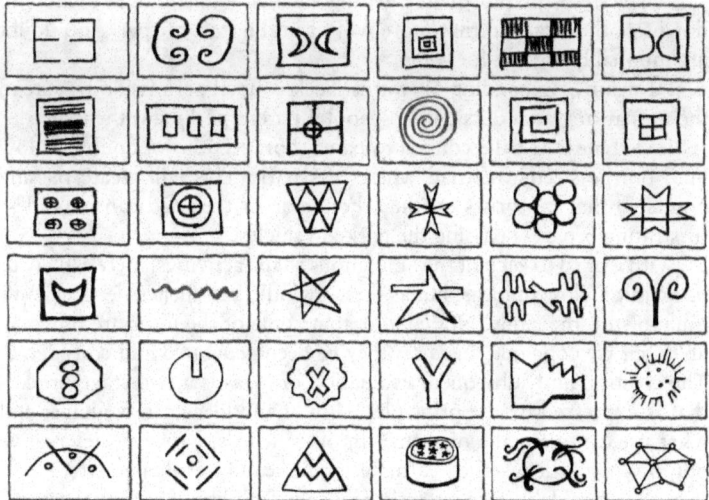

Figure 2.2 This selection of abstract ambiguous shapes extends the challenge set in Figure 2.1.

classroom, the school, the neighbourhood, the country or even be global. Tell the children that one or more of the shapes can point towards solutions; that the game is a variation of the 'What could it be? What does it remind you of?'

As soon as you show the grid to the class, children will subconsciously interpret the shapes and link them with the aim in mind of offering solutions to the stated problem and once again, the 'don't try too hard, don't judge yet' principle applies.

As an example, let's use the problem of long rows of cars parked on the road outside the school gates at dropping-off and picking-up time, an issue in our village. This causes frustration when drivers have to wait for oncoming traffic to pass. The parked cars are also a potential source of danger at the start and end of the day since they cut down visibility. What can be done about it?

6/1 Connected points – Organise a car sharing scheme, a network of drivers, so that fewer cars park outside the school.

1/1 Lines like pointers – Suggest that parents park farther away from the school and walk with their children. If teacher parking is the issue, the shape suggests enlarging the car park into the adjoining school field.

2/3 Wiggly line – Varying the start and finish time for different years. This would mean that not all of the staff arrived at school at the start of the day, and the same would apply to parents. How could this be achieved without disrupting the school day? Do any of our abstract shapes offer possible solutions?

4/6 Nested squares/squares getting smaller – Encourage teachers to downsize their cars so that more will fit in the staff car park (no doubt an impossibly big ask for some).

1/1 again – Expanding outwards. Seek council permission to extend the no-parking area outside the school if parent parking is the issue.

1/5 – Lines. Ask the council to paint short sections of double yellow lines on the stretch of road where cars park. This will create passing points so that motorists on the school side of the road can make less frustrating progress passing the parked vehicles.

With regard to each of the ambiguous shape activities, there's likely to be an initial flow of ideas, but as these dwindle and silences lengthen, it's time to stop the game. Notice, too, that some of the ideas are unworkable, but we conclude this *after* they've been generated and considered. The creation and subsequent evaluation of ideas is a two-stage process that is expressed by the principle; 'How many ideas can we have, and what use can we make of them?' In other words, we have the creative outpouring of ideas – the raw material that can be evaluated later – and then the more deliberate analysis of the workability of each suggestion.

Another important principle is that no idea is ever wasted. Even if an idea does not seem to work or apply at the time, encourage children not

Questioning and Creativity 35

to discard it. As a writer, Steve is an inveterate note-maker and scribbles down ideas as they come to him. Sometimes, he looks back through his notebooks or computer files and reviews old ideas, some of which might have been in limbo for months or even years. Happily, it's often the case that an idea that didn't seem to be going anywhere at the time now offers fresh insight and a sense of direction for further thinking. A more subtle point is that keeping and valuing all the ideas we have amounts to an act of self-respect, a kind of self-thanking for the creative fecundity of the mind.

Activity: Symbols

The word symbol comes from Ancient Greek, meaning a sign through which we infer something. These days, the words symbol and sign are used differently: a symbol is rich in meaning and association, whereas a sign – a road sign, for example – conveys an immediate simple message. You might emphasise this point to children by showing them different road signs and asking them if they can immediately pick out what they mean. Extend the activity by showing the class some symbols, such as Figure 2.3. Begin by inviting short descriptions of the symbols

Figure 2.3 Children are shown these well-known symbols and are asked to suggest what they could represent.

themselves, then go on to encourage children to suggest what they *might* mean. What we're looking for here is not necessarily the right answer (though some children might know it in some cases) but a variety of interpretations. A variation of the activity is to encourage children to ask questions about the symbols rather than just guessing at their meanings, although an educated guess, one based on a reason or reasons, would be acceptable.

If children have difficulty working out any symbol's meaning, you can offer them some prompts –

1. Olympic rings represent the five continents and the coming together of athletes from around the world.
2. The world tree. This is an ancient symbol representing the joining of the earth, the heavens and the underworld.
3. Mars, the Roman god of war. The symbol is a shield and a spear.
4. The mathematical symbol of infinity. As an extension to this, you could show the class other and perhaps more familiar maths symbols – addition, subtraction, division, equals, etc. and ask for ideas about why they take the form they do.
5. The peace symbol. It combines the semaphore letters N and D, which in turn stand for nuclear disarmament. Put together, they symbolise both peace and hope.
6. The caduceus. The word derives from ancient Greek and means a herald or public messenger. The design has long been a symbol of medicine and the medical profession, originating with Asclepius, who was revered by the ancient Greeks as the god of healing and whose cult involved the use of snakes. The symbol appears on some medical alert bracelets and pendants.
7. The triskelion or triskele, the word coming again from the Greek meaning 'three times'. Some sources have it that the three joined spirals represent the three elements of earth, air and water, while others believe it derives from the three aspects of the Triple Goddess in Celtic mythology; maiden, mother and crone.
8. Yin Yang. These represent the two complementary principles in Chinese philosophy; yin is negative, dark and feminine while yang is positive, bright and masculine (it would be interesting to see if any children raise the topic of sexism at this point). The interaction between the two opposites is thought to maintain the harmony and balance of the universe.

A variation is to show the class the flags of different nations and, again, invite questioning around the symbolic meaning of them.

Animals too have symbolic qualities, often expressed as similes. So we have as cunning as a fox, as gentle as a dove, as mad as a March hare, as quiet as a mouse and many others. Children are likely to find linking these qualities with their respective creatures easier than thinking about the symbols mentioned previously, so you might consider using this activity as a precursor to the more challenging ones.

Another 'route in' to the concept of symbolism is to look at emojis, with which the children are likely to be familiar. A number of sources assert that emojis (from the Japanese for picture and character) are symbols, although they're often also called icons, from the Greek for likeness or image. The emotions that many emojis represent are obvious, but you can challenge the class by showing less familiar ones or by offering the class a list of less common emotions and asking the children to design emojis around them. A variation is to invite children to design subtly different emojis for similar emotions, such as envy and jealousy, happiness and joy, irritation and annoyance, etc.

Activity: Love Is

You may be too young to know about the 'Love is . . .' comic strip that was created by New Zealand cartoonist Kim Casali in the 1960s, who drew the romantic cartoons for her future husband. Examples are readily found online.

A more testing variation of 'the mind is like a river' on page 37 is to use thoughts and thinking rather than 'the mind' more generally. Go through the same process as in the linked activity. Take it further by presenting the class with some pictures, perhaps the abstract shapes in Figure 2.2 and ask the children to think of them as metaphors or similes. So, 'A thought is . . .' or 'Thinking is like . . .' The game also makes use of 'because', a 'sticky' word, since children have to tag a reason on to their ideas – the mind is like a spider web because it connects up different thoughts.

A similar idea can be used to encourage children's understanding of other abstract concepts and also to prompt some creative writing.

Activity: Switching Domains

Another technique for problem-solving is to take a problem in one area or domain and then look in another area for insights and possible solutions. For instance, when scientists and engineers at the American Space Agency NASA wanted to design tough little robot probes to explore Mars, they talked with biologists at the local zoo's insect house. Insects are tough and have huge variety and move about in different ways, so discussing them with the experts provided plenty of ideas for the subsequent design of robot vehicles. You can use this example to test the children's creativity. Explain what conditions are like on the Moon or

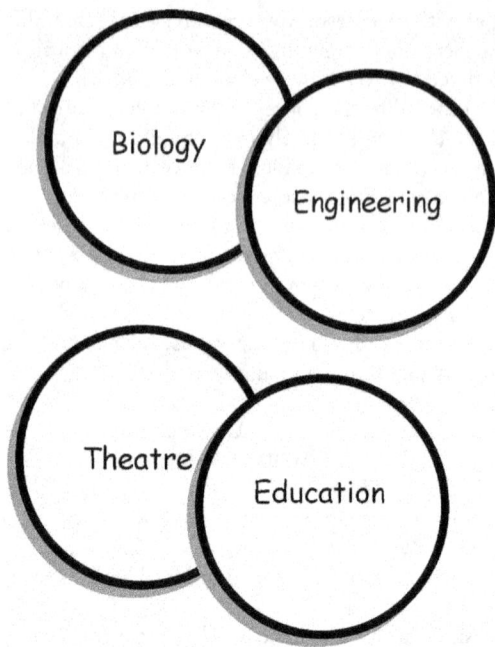

Figure 2.4 Another way to solve problems in one context is to look at another context for insights.

Mars, explain that we would like to send roving robot probes there and then show children pictures of insects to see if any of their features could form the basis of the design of a probe.

Perhaps a more immediately accessible example would be to look at problems to do with your school and talk with the class about the way, for example, theatres are run with the aim of solving school-based problems. One way of preparing the discussion is to have children brainstorm terms connected with the theatre and have these on display while the discussion takes place. Or you might choose to supply a list of words, explain terms the children don't understand and then invite children to add to the list.

So, to summarise, as illustrated in Figure 2.4 –

Identify a problem to do with school (not necessarily your own).
Look at the way theatres are run.
Check for correspondences between well-run theatres and the school problem.
Discuss how the school problem might be resolved, given these fresh insights.

Activity: Odd One Out

Another game that makes use of creative connecting developed out of the familiar odd-one-out technique that's been around for decades. So, if we have beech, violet, fern, orchid and pine, test the children's thinking by asking them to suggest a reason as to why *each* of the examples could be the odd one out.

Take the game further by showing the class several lists and inviting the children to link two or more items from different lists –

Beech, violet, fern, orchid, pine,

Gold, glass, bronze, iron, slate.

Town, city, village, Utopia, suburb.

Tea, cola, beer, water, coffee.

Carpenter, miner, teacher, barber, electrician.

Ant, bear, cat, eel, fox.

CREATE

This acronym sums up the usefulness of questioning in more fully exploiting children's ability to think both creatively and critically. Keeping the CREATE process in mind means that children can bring an open-minded scepticism to the information they encounter: they need not be dogmatic themselves but also not vulnerable to the dogmas of others, especially as these are often expressed with clever rhetorical and persuasive language. So, CREATE means –

C – Connect – making initial links seeing the big picture prior to assimilating information.
R – Relate – owning the knowledge and assessing its relevance, including to oneself personally.
E – Explore – notice and question, probe more deeply.
A – Analyse – step back, think critically and evaluate.
T – Transform – encourage further insights, make plans and build strategies.
E – Experience – look at outcomes and consequences, modify as necessary and begin thinking of the next project. Also, enjoy the pleasant experience of having ideas.

Some teachers we've met have made a large wall poster so that children are continually reminded of what the creative attitude entails.

3 A Medley of Question-generating Activities

The previous section has aimed to highlight the value of questioning in the classroom, both from the teacher's and pupils' points of view; to look at the impediments to developing a 'questioning classroom', and to offer specific techniques and activities for boosting children's self-confidence as it relates to creative and critical thinking through the enquiry process.

This section, as the heading suggests, presents a range of ideas for opening out the kinds of questioning children can do. The activities can be used flexibly – as warmups to sessions from the previous section or as a build-up to the more challenging and extended activities that appear in the rest of the book.

The activities here are loosely sequenced in order of their sophistication but can also be selected to suit your particular requirements.

Activity: Getting-to-know-you Questions

This is an easy, fun activity when you have a new class. Prepare a bingo sheet for each child or write up a list of questions that children can pick from. Or, indeed, they can make up their own. Children then move around the classroom, crossing off questions when they find a classmate who would answer the question in the same way: the classmate can also sign the question to verify it's been answered in the affirmative. Once a pupil has completed a sheet, they can return to their place and read and write in their ideas journal (page 131) or another activity that you've prepared. Questions can include –

I have a brother – do you? (Or I have a sister and brother, two brothers, etc.)

I enjoy nature programmes on TV – do you?

Do you like heights? I don't!

DOI: 10.4324/9781003608714-3

A Medley of Question-generating Activities 41

My favourite colour is blue – what's yours?
I really like cats. What's your favourite pet?
I'm not a vegetarian, but I like vegetables better than meat. What about you?

A variation of the activity is to have classmates simply ask each other questions from children's prepared lists. Responders are invited to give reasons for their replies. Example questions include –

What's your favourite colour (or food, drink, TV programme, etc.) and why?
If you could go on holiday anywhere in the world, where would that be? Why do you like the place so much?
If you could meet any character from film, TV, stories or comics, who would that be? If you could ask that character three questions, what would they be? Why did you choose those questions?
If you could be any animal for a day, what would you choose to be and why?

Activity: Picture Masking

Crop a picture so that it becomes ambiguous and then encourage children to ask questions about it. So, using the example in Figure 3.1, questions might include –

- How would you describe the expression on the woman's face?
- Where is she going or where has she come from?
- Who might she be waving to?
- What might be the reason for her journey?
- What would we expect to see in the full picture?

Activity: What Is . . . ?

Each child is given a blank sheet of paper and chooses an animal or plant appended to the question 'What is . . . ?' The sheets are then passed around the class systematically (so that children don't get the same sheet repeatedly) and children write a brief answer. Alternatively, each child chooses a plant or animal and writes the question in their ideas journal. The teacher or another child nominates someone to ask their question and the other children respond by writing their answers down. Then,

Figure 3.1 Children are shown part of a picture and are encouraged to ask questions about it, including what might lie beyond the frame.

a selection of responses can be shared. Responses might be scientific, personal, poetical, etc.

So, for example, what is a cat?
A ball of fur that likes a warm lap
A common domestic pet
Something that eats, sleeps and purrs
Mouse chaser
A whiskered bundle of love

Activity: Question Flip

The aim here is for pairs of children to use questions asked by one to formulate a question by the other child in the pair. So if a child asks, 'What's your favourite food?' the other child, after answering, might then ask, 'What's your favourite drink?' You can introduce and explain the activity by showing the class a list of questions and asking what the flip or flips might be. In many cases, there can be more than one way of flipping a question. So 'What's your favourite food?' could be flipped into – 'What's your least favourite food?' 'What food do you eat most often?' 'What's the most exotic food you've ever eaten?' 'Where is your favourite place to eat out?'

Activity: Twenty Questions

This well-known game is ideal for getting children to ask questions. The basic idea is to have a volunteer pick an animal, plant, object, etc. The other children then ask questions to try and find out what it is. Guesses are only allowed if a child can explain the reasoning behind it. You can increase the challenge by specifying that the class only has 19 questions next time, then 18 and so on, though obviously you can't specify so few questions that the task becomes impossible. One way of making the activity easier is to use one of the grids (pages 87 and 90). This limits the choices to 36 items. Tell the children that questions such as 'Is it on the top row?', or 'Is it in the right-hand column?' are not allowed. You might also consider writing relevant vocabulary around the grids and encourage children to incorporate such terms into their questions. Follow up the session by discussing with the class which were the most insightful and searching questions and why. Yes-no questions are also called surface questions that don't reveal much information. More open questions are also called 'digging' questions that delve beneath the surface to uncover more information. These are different terms for what are more familiarly known as closed and open questions.

As a variation of the twenty questions activity, children can follow up a closed question with an open one. So –

Is it an animal? Yes.

Where in the world does the animal live?

In this case, you can reduce the number of questions the class can ask the questionee because open questions generate more information and give greater clues. You can also alternate closed and open questions.

Activity: A Mini Mystery

Present children with this puzzler and invite them to question you in order to try to solve it. The solution follows after – so that you don't find yourself puzzled.

Imagine a room locked from the outside. The French door on to the balcony is open and the curtain, partly drawn across, is flapping wildly in the wind. The table by the window has nothing on it. There is water on the carpet and also broken glass. Romeo and Juliet are lying dead nearby. What might have happened?

The scenario is that Romeo and Juliet are goldfish (you can talk to the class about making assumptions later). They were happily swimming in their goldfish bowl on the table when a strong gust of wind swept the bowl off the table, shattering it on the floor. You can add the details that the owner of the fish popped out and locked the door but forgot to close the French door.

If mysteries like these appeal to you and the children, we recommend 'Whodunits; more than 100 mysteries for you to solve', while 'The Detective's Handbook', written for children, is full of interesting information about detecting; a useful addition, we think, to the work you do with the class on thinking skills. See Bibliography.

Activity: Toggle

Present children with a list of statements and ask children to turn them into questions and vice versa. The value of this activity, as well as highlighting the difference, is to help create a mindset where statements need not be accepted as they stand: once children get into the habit of turning received facts into questions, they are more likely to challenge information they encounter but also think of other linked questions to ask. You'll note, by the way, that this exercise overlaps with the London-is-the-capital-of-England activity mentioned earlier, where the most obvious 'flip' is to ask, 'Why is London the capital of England?'

In his (to some) controversial book 'The Science Delusion', the maverick biologist Rupert Sheldrake takes what he regards to be ten dogmatic statements that underpin the current materialistic paradigm of science and turns them into questions, which he then goes on to explore. So, for instance, he has chapter headings that include; 'Are the laws of nature fixed?' 'Is all biological inheritance material?' 'Are minds confined to brains?' and 'Is nature purposeless?'

Our reaction to these questions casts light on our own belief system. We've come across people who are outraged by such questions and dismiss them out of hand (thus sharing the materialistic world view of much of science), while others are prepared – as is Sheldrake – to look at the evidence either way and come to their own conclusions. For us, Rupert Sheldrake's willingness to question prevailing assumptions has the same subversive flavour as the general tone of Postman and Weingartner's 'Teaching as a Subversive Activity'. However, to be clear, questioning received wisdom is not necessarily to disagree with it but serves to test its veracity – what evidence or proof supports it?

We explore this topic more fully in 'Understanding the World Through Narrative.' Also, if the kinds of bold questions – questions that challenge the scientific mainstream – Sheldrake asks interest you, you can find a number of his talks on YouTube.

See also 'This Is the Answer – What Are the Questions?' activity on page 66.

Activity: What Might Happen Next?

This activity calls on children to both speculate and infer – explaining their reasoning when they do this. There are many permutations, from the very simple to the much more complex, so you can increase the challenge each time. Examples you might use include –

Offer a simple rhyming poem with the rhyme missing and ask children to decide which words should be there.

Show the class one or more pages from a comic book and ask them which panels might follow.

Read most of a very short story and ask the class how it could end.

Show an appropriate video clip, pause and invite ideas about what might happen next.

We've also found that many children enjoy offering classmates their own examples.

Activity: Questioning So-called Nonsense Words

The following poem is inspired by Lewis Carroll's 'Jabberwocky'. The task is to invite children to consider what the supposedly nonsensical words might mean by asking them to get a 'sense' of them. This is as much intuitive as it is based on reasoning. However, some words – onomatopoeic words, for example – convey a strong sense of what they intend to communicate. So, for us, the word 'thud' is heavy, indicating something quite large and flattish or rounded being dropped, like a cannonball dropping into the mud and not breaking or shattering when it hits the surface. 'Splash' is a 'liquidy' word that we group together with splish, splosh, sploosh, spulash, splat and splatter. Ask children if they get different impressions as they say these words. For instance, 'splish' for us creates the impression of something quite small being dropped into shallow water or walking through a shallow puddle, while 'spulash' or 'sploosh' is something heavier dropped into deeper water.

Something Comes By

It was a roiling night
of glombous reebs and grasting storm.
Barb owls huddled out the swirlwind's bite;
Decapedes in their hollows snoodled warm.

All through the low and high
of Shadowland the streams ran churdling
in the forest deeps. Moon's houring
sent out abalone light above the cloud hills hurdling,
while from the screamsome north –
the ice-teeth scouring
and breathly deathly cold came wreathing with a sigh.

Then
Something nudged and trudged aside the trees
and tramped the gladeland paths to squeshy mire;
made the seed-balloons pop and the opticus cry
as, in its thousand eyes,
the stars lay mirrored in the direful sky
and weepydrops crystalled red as vulcan fire.

Something comes this way
– goes by
something gaart and vast and sleez,
that sends the night mare riding
and the dawnflower fearfully hiding
as it passes, leaves its shadow
on the road to midnight seas.

Some words or phrases are not completely nonsensical and may convey a clear meaning immediately, such as Shadowland, barb owl, opticus and dawnflower. Ask children to notice what comes to mind as you slowly reread these words to them. Also, take a word like 'squeshy' and ask for words that the children are reminded of by it – squish, squash, quash, squeeze. Further, ask if these indicate dryness or not – many children will say they do not, that in fact they suggest wetness and also pressure, like squeezing a sponge.

Another way of using the vocabulary of the poem is to point out how the same word can be used as different parts of speech – so 'crystalled' in the poem is used as a verb, while Vulcan, usually used as a noun to name the god of fire, is here used as an adjective.

A further activity is to look at combined words: what do screamsome, gladeland and dawnflower suggest? Some word combinations form a common thread in our language, such as skyscraper, bookworm, tree-hugger, showstopper, spine-tingling, bloodcurdling, ear-piercing and pencil-pusher.

Activity: Kennings

Looking at word pairings like these naturally leads to a study of kennings – a figure of speech using word combinations in place of a single word, commonly involving alliteration and assonance. Here for example is a kenning poem about a woodpecker –

> Tree tapper, grub grabber, writhing-maggot muncher,
> bright blood-red woodland dweller . . .
>
> Fresh grass-green-leaf hunter, spotted soarer,
> flying fantasy flapping furiously,
> feathery featured, glisten-eyed small-speckled songster . . .

Kennings were often created by the Anglo-Saxons and Norse cultures, frequently in the form of riddles. The well-known Angle-Saxon poem 'Beowulf' is packed with them, such as; slaughter-pole (spear), ring-giver (king), ring-hoard (dragon's treasure) and battle-fire (dragon's fiery breath).

Once children get the hang of kennings, present them with a list of common objects and invite kenning-like word combinations. Examples we've come across include – pencil (wordmaker), car (road-roller), computer (fact-finder), cat (mouse-pouncer), dog (tail-wagger), sun (light-giver) and school (fact-hoard).

For younger pupils – we're thinking upper KS2 – the stories in 'Wordhoard: Anglo-Saxon stories for young people' by Jill Paton Walsh and Kevin Crossley-Holland contain examples of the gritty and almost physical language we've been talking about. For older pupils, we would recommend writer-translator Michael Alexander's translation of Beowulf and his book 'The Earliest English Poems.' In the poem 'The Ruin', we find powerful word combinations like rooftrees, gatetowers, showershields, gravesgrasp, wallbase, gold-bright, mood-glad and war-gear.

More challenging 'physical' language can be found in the poetry of the Victorian Jesuit priest Gerard Manley-Hopkins (one of our favourite poets). In his poem 'Felix Randal', for example, we find beautiful phrases such as – mould of man, big-boned and hardy-handsome. Also, the superb lines (Randal was a farrier recently deceased) – 'When thou at the random grim forge, powerful amidst peers,/Dids't fettle for the great grey drayhorse his bright and battering sandal!' You can almost hear and feel the hammer banging down on the red-hot metal. The edition we quote from (see Bibliography) has a very useful introduction by the academic W. H. Gardner.

A fascinating but controversial hypothesis in linguistics is called phonosemantics or sound symbolism, which is a link between word sounds and the concepts they refer to. In a fascinating book called 'Gods in the Word', programmer and computational linguist Margaret Magnus points out that the phoneme 'str' suggests linearity as in strip, strap, string, street and stroll, while 'gl' suggests light and light hitting certain surfaces such as gleam, glimmer, glitter, glisten and maybe glance and glow. Examples such as these are also called phonesthemes, where a sound suggests a meaning.

Activity: Bouba-kiki

An interesting activity to run with the children is known as the 'bouba-kiki effect'. Show the class two shapes, one curvy and rounded like a cloud, the other spiky like a skewed, many-pointed star. Explain to the children that one of these is called a kiki and the other is a bouba (these being made-up nonsense words). Ask the children to decide which is which. You'll likely find that the majority of children label the rounded shape as a bouba and the spiky shape as a kiki (https://en.wikipedia.org/wiki/Bouba/kiki_effect). Ask the children how they know. Many will mime round or spiky shapes in the air as they explain and some may even tell you about rounded and stick-like letters in the words that helped them to decide. You can then point out – or they may do it for you – that many words referring to round things have rounded letters – bubble, ball, globe, balloon, round. And many words referring to spiky things have sticking-out letters and refer to stick-like things – stick, pike, pin, pick (axe), peak, point.

The website Lancaster.ac.uk (specifically www.lancaster.ac.uk/fass/projects/stylistics/topic5a/7soundchecksheet.htm#:) delves deeply into this subject, pointing out at the start of the article that the words 'incy' and 'wincy' in the poem 'incy wincy spider' don't just indicate smallness but seem to symbolise it. This led us to wonder if other smallness words are phonosemantically linked – teeny, tiny, minute, mini, miniature, little, weeny, titchy, dinky and maybe even Lilliputian.

Activity: Question Ripple

Children can work in pairs or small groups. One child offers a simple statement and then others in the group ask questions about it, a kind of rippling out of the topic. So – I like reading? What kinds of books do you like reading? What is your favourite book? Do you read non-fiction? What subject(s) do you prefer?

Take it further: Compile a list of subjects to run the question ripple activity – TV, food, drinks, games, etc. Ask the children to help you compile a list.

Activity: Synaesthesia

This word comes from the Greek and means a bringing together, or a cross-matching, of the senses. Here, one sensory impression is expressed in terms of another. By way of explaining this, look at this list of words – aggressive, backbone, big, coarse, dry, fat, green, hot, rough, smooth, velvety. What they have in common is that they're all terms used by wine tasters.

At the extreme end of the synaesthesia spectrum, a person who perceives, say, sound as a taste, might actually experience that taste upon hearing the associated sound. Although some commentators have it that synaesthesia is a 'harmless neurological condition', it can bring great benefits. Go online and type 'how synaesthesia inspires artists' to find out more.

For most people, at the very least, inviting them to cross-match sensory modes challenges the imagination and gives children a fresh way of describing things in their creative writing. Again, type 'synaesthesia in poetry or literature' to find some fascinating examples.

As a questioning activity, list the five senses on the board and ask children to volunteer questions such as –

If bright red was a smell, what smell would it be?
If the sound of thunder was a texture, what would it feel like?
If the feel of sandpaper was a colour, what would it be?

Activity: What Is It Like to Be . . . ?

Another activity to challenge the imagination and encourage questioning is to ask one or more children to pretend to be an animal or a plant – in their imaginations as a visualisation, not as a mime, unless they really want to. Other children then question the 'imagineers'. Start the process by choosing a familiar animal first, say a cat. You might also offer some facts about the thing chosen. For instance, a cat's sense of smell is 14 times better than that of humans (www.pawschicago.org/). So, questions could be about what a cat can smell that people can't. Incidentally, if you've run the 'Synaesthesia' activity with the class (page 49), children might talk about a smell in terms of colour, sound or texture.

After a few minutes, pick another group to choose a different living thing. You can extend the activity by suggesting that children choose non-living things, such as a cloud, a mountain, a river, etc.

As an aside, the philosopher Thomas Nagel once asked, 'What is it like to be a bat?', pointing out that to know is impossible since we can only know what it is like to be ourselves and, by extension, know something of other fellow humans through shared experience. If you search the reference online, you'll find a raft of academic articles on Nagel's assertion. That said, asking children to imagine being an animal, plant or object prompts them to gather up what they know about it and see the world from a different point of view – another valuable aspect of creative thinking.

Activity: Questions Around a Theme

Pick a theme, for example, dreams. And invite children to come up with questions related to it. Pupils can question one child, a small group of volunteers or each question can be directed at the whole class to harvest a variety of answers. So –

What is the most vivid dream you remember?

Do you have any thoughts about why we dream?

Do you dream in colour?

Do any people you know appear in your dreams?

Do any of your dreams relate to what's going on in your life?

Do you have recurring dreams or themes that crop up in different dreams?

Why do we call them dreams anyway?

Martin Luther King Jr said 'I have a dream', by which he meant a vision for a better, brighter future. It was a call for freedom and equality. Do you think this could ever be achieved and if so, how, and if not, why not?

Such questions can act as springboards for further questions that broaden out the topic –

Is dreaming the same mental state as daydreaming?

Why are nightmares so called?

A Medley of Question-generating Activities   51

How do we know when someone is dreaming?

We've heard that lucid dreaming is when someone knows they're dreaming and can control where the dream goes. Can anyone here do that?

Activity: Thought-provoking Questions

Initially, pick a question that children will most likely need to reflect on. They need not make their thoughts public, but they could write them out in their ideas journals. Examples of such questions include –

Is it better to live to a ripe old age with little excitement or lead an adventurous but shorter life?

What does it mean to be free?

If you could take away all negative feelings, would this be a good or bad thing?

Is everyone's life of equal value, or is it more important to protect some lives rather than others? (See also the 'Lifeboat Dilemma' on page 102).

What wise advice do you wish you had followed, if any? Or, what is the wisest thing you've ever read, seen or been told to you? Why do you think this?

Tip: If you search online for 'thought-provoking questions for children', you'll find plenty of further examples.

Activity: Faction

This is a term we use when questions are generated that mix fact and fiction. Here you see that we use the 'what if' technique to create questions, which are themselves a kind of thought experiment that can lead to further questions, discussions, debates and even philosophical enquiries. Here are some examples, though of course invite children to contribute further ideas.

1. What if all roads became toll roads?
2. What if all large mammals except humans became extinct?
3. What if a new law was passed in this country limiting parents to one child from now on?
4. What if the law changed so that wealth was distributed equally through society and everyone was paid the same wage regardless of the job they did?

5. What if every child could choose what they learned at school?
6. What if pocket AI mobile phones became the voice of our conscience?

You'll appreciate that questions like these, while they may never become reality, form a rich source of further questions and discussion around real-life issues. Question one, for instance, centres on the environment, financial inequalities in society and how far a government should dictate the population's degree of freedom. The issues around question five focus on 'child centred education' with a twist, a topic thoroughly explored and powerfully argued in 'Teaching as a Subversive Activity' – see Bibliography.

Activity: Please, Mr Einstein

Talking of thought experiments, one of the most famous came from the theoretical physicist Albert Einstein, who wondered what the universe would look like if you could speed along beside a light beam. The insights he gained helped him to formulate his theories of relativity.

The idea behind this activity is to pick a character, real or fictitious, or even an animal and invite children to make lists of questions to ask their chosen character/animal if this is possible. Encourage pertinent and searching questions rather than 'What's your favourite colour?' or similar. So –

Please Mr T-rex – How do you manage with such small arms? What happens when you fall down? Do you teach your babies to be as fierce as you are or are they born that way? Do you ever fight with other meat-eating dinosaurs? What was it like back in dinosaur times?

Please Mr Armstrong (Neil Armstrong, the first man on the moon) – How did you get picked to be the first person to step out onto the moon? How did you move wearing such a bulky space suit? What's life like in a cramped spaceship? How did you decide what to say when you took your first step onto the moon? How did the people in charge of the mission choose the other astronauts (Buzz Aldrin and Michael Collins) to travel with you?

Some of the answers can be discovered through research, while others might well remain tantalisingly forever unknown.

Activity: Context Sentences

The aim here is to offer the class a vague sentence to prompt questions that aim to create a more detailed context. The activity serves as

A Medley of Question-generating Activities 53

a prompt for questions but also a springboard for creating ideas prior to story-making.

So – Andrews lay slumped on the sofa.

Who is Andrews?

Is Andrews a man, woman or child?

What state is Andrews in – asleep, dead, drunk, knocked out or just resting? (In answer to the question 'What state is Andrews in?' one child said 'California'. We gave him a merit mark.)

Where is the sofa?

What has happened to cause Andrews to be 'slumped' on the sofa?

What might happen now?

All Jackie saw was the strange glow of its eyes.

Who is Jackie?

How old is she, and what does she look like?

What is the thing she saw?

Why do its eyes have a strange glow?

Is the glow literal or some kind of metaphor, as in 'the angry glow in its eyes', or something supernatural?

Are they actually eyes – could Jackie be mistaken?

Where is Jackie?

What has happened beforehand to bring her here?

What might happen now?

This activity can be combined with the 'Counter-flip' game (page 72), whereby children toss a two-colour counter to obtain yes or no answers and or the 'Add-a-bit' technique on page 82. This will further enrich the context. By way of guidance, suggest to the class that counter-flip questions could be genre-based if working pairs or small groups prefer. So if a group chooses Science Fiction, further questions could be – 'Do the eyes belong to an alien?' 'Do the eyes belong to a robot?' or 'Is the 'owner' of the glowing eyes hostile?'

If using the activity as a basis for story-making, ask children to draw a beginning-middle-end narrative line and decide where in the story Jones was slumped on the sofa or where Jackie saw the glowing eyes. Invite children to pick other points along the line and think of questions that begin to develop a more fleshed-out narrative. Counter-flip answers obtained earlier can provide insights into asking further questions. So for example, if the glowing eyes belonged to a robot, children might want to find out if a scientist on Earth built it, if that scientist was a good guy or a bad guy, what purpose the robot serves etc.

Activity: Structure and Function

Point out that these two are related. Firstly, show the class some simple everyday objects, such as a selection of spoons and ask children to *really* notice how structure is related to function: it's quite likely that none of the children will ever have thought about this before, but rather they might have taken spoons completely for granted. Follow up by inviting children to ask questions about spoons and related objects, such as –

Do we know who invented the spoon?

Was the spoon invented once, and then the idea spread, or did different people in different parts of the world have the same idea?

Why is it called a spoon? (We find that the word comes from the Old English 'spon' meaning 'chip'. Can the children suggest what a chip might mean and how it relates to the design of a spoon?)

Was the fork invented at the same time as the spoon?

Why is it called a fork?

Do all forks have the same number of prongs?

Did the idea of the pitchfork come out of the invention of the fork you eat with?

Move on by asking children to notice objects in the classroom and to carry out the same activity – how is structure related to function? Develop the activity by posing further questions and/or inviting children to come up with their own, such as –

Why do giraffes have long necks?

Why do many types of cactus have thick, waxy cuticles?

Why do cats have whiskers?

Why do dandelion seeds have fluffy tops?

Why do zebras have stripes?

In some cases answers will be obvious, but if not either encourage the children to do some research or speculate on possible answers that can be checked later.

A Medley of Question-generating Activities 55

Activity: The 'Who Am I?' Game

Prepare a number of sticky notes or cards that name people known to the children; celebrities perhaps, characters from fiction etc. The basic game places a sticky note on a volunteer's forehead and then that child has to question the rest of the class about who the mystery person might be. There can be more than one volunteer each time, with two or three children in a team having the same person named on their foreheads. The teacher stands by to supply any answers that the rest of the children in the class don't know and/or you can nominate a small team of researchers to look up answers if nobody knows.

The game can be competitive, with the child or team asking the fewest questions to identify the named person as the winner, although competitiveness need not come into it. More useful, in our opinion, is that questions from several rounds of the game are recorded and then discussed to decide which were the most incisive in uncovering the mystery persons.

Note: If a child doesn't want a sticky note on his forehead, write the name on a piece of paper and hold it up for the class to see while standing behind and to the side of the questioner(s).

A variation of the activity is to extend it into the 'What Am I?' game, where animals, plants and inanimate objects are included. This is similar to the 'Animal, Vegetable or Mineral' TV show, where more information about it can be found on Wikipedia. Examples can be taken from a topic that the class is currently studying and can thus serve as a useful revision of related terms and concepts. You might even pin up relevant vocabulary on a display board for easy instant access.

Activity: Question Wall

Set aside some wall space and invite children to pin up questions, perhaps around a topic that the class is studying, one that you have chosen or other areas of enquiry that interest the children. Pictures, quotes, facts, subsidiary questions, suggestions for research strategies, etc. can also be included. This makes the display more interesting and can also serve to generate further questions. If you run this activity, children should by then understand that pinning up questions is not a sign of ignorance but an expression of curiosity and the desire to find out more – as we've mentioned earlier, but do so again because the point is so important.

As a side note; 'ignorant' is a loaded word. Synonyms include uneducated and unlearned but also rude and ill-mannered. These connotations should be avoided. The word itself derives from Latin and originally means simply 'not knowing'. Since all the children (and adults) in all schools have limited knowledge when set against the constantly expanding sum-total of human knowledge*, we are all 'not knowing' to a greater or lesser degree – back to the notion of Bloom's Taxonomy and 'full understanding' on page 17.

*We checked online at the expansion rate of human knowledge and were presented with various estimates – an object lesson in not taking facts at face value.

As a rounding-off to the question wall activity, time should be set aside for some discussion of answers (and further questions arising). The topics that have been explored are then removed and the question wall refreshed.

Activity: Knock On

This activity is about exploring the consequences if something suddenly changes in the world. It shares some similarities with 'what if', and like that activity can focus on any subject area and/or form the basis for developing narratives.

Begin the activity by posing a knock-on question such as –

What would be the knock-on effects of a valuable metal running out?

What would the consequences be if scientists developed a drug that allowed people to live to be 150?

What if increasingly serious climate change meant that travel for pleasure was banned worldwide?

What if a computer super virus wiped all hard drives today?

Once a question has been asked, invite the class to gather further ideas, which may be in the form of more questions. To help with this, ideas can be grouped under a number of headings that can be displayed on the board – the home, industry, transport, art etc.

So if copper suddenly ran out –

Would the government recall copper coins so that the metal could be put to other uses?

Similarly, would it be worth replacing the copper pipes in our houses with some other material?

Would bronze statues (copper and tin alloy) be melted down to recover the copper?

Activity: The Why Game

Some years ago, Steve collaborated with educationalist Sara Stanley on a book called 'But Why?' that aimed to show adults how to teach young children to think philosophically. 'Why' is one of the big open questions that children should be encouraged to ask. The 'why game' invites children to write out such questions on scraps of paper, preferably ones that really do intrigue them, to be drawn at random from an envelope or to display on a board. As time permits, pick a question and invite the class to discuss possible answers and/or do some research to find out. There's no shame in not knowing the answers – we live in a world of not knowing. This is easily demonstrated by pointing out that although we use words constantly, very few people are likely to know where they come from. Take, for instance, the words teacher, pupil, adult, child – although we know what these words mean, *why* is a teacher so called or a pupil so called? We didn't know until we spent five minutes online and discovered that teacher comes from Proto-Germanic meaning 'to show'; pupil comes from Latin and originally referred to a child who was an orphan under the care of a guardian; adult is again from Latin and means 'to grow to maturity'; and child comes from the Old English 'cild', meaning an infant (but where does the word infant come from?). As an aside, one of the most beautiful word origins, in our opinion, refers to astronaut, meaning 'star sailor' or 'sailor to the stars'. Delving into the etymology of words can throw up insights into related words. So from 'astro', we get astronomy, astrology (we wonder what the difference of the word endings means), astral and astrolabe. From 'naut', we are pointed towards nautical and nautilus. Taking some time to study the etymology of words* also encourages the use of a dictionary and a thesaurus. Thinking back, we don't recall any teacher actually telling us that the origins of words can usually be found in square brackets at the end of a definition in a dictionary. Nor, as shy youngsters, did we have the wit or the confidence to ask about it.

*Etymology, by the way, derives from the Greek meaning 'the true sense or sense of a truth' and the suffix 'logia' meaning the study of logic (from 'logos' meaning reason). 'Word' has its roots in Proto-Germanic, meaning to say or to speak.

You can kickstart the why game by offering the class some intriguing questions of your own. Teachers we've spoken to have given us –

Why does the sun rise and set?
Why don't we have insects the size of elephants?
Why do we have different languages in the world?

Why do we need water in order for life to begin and evolve?
Why do I have feelings, even if I'm only remembering past incidents?
Why do we have sleep and dreams?

Activity: Etymology

Extend the 'Why' game by giving individual children or small groups some words to research, which provides insights into how our language develops. Also, many word origins offer a concrete and more memorable way of understanding abstract concepts. For example, the words calculate and calculus are derived from Latin *calculus*, a small pebble used in counting, such as on an abacus... We find such research compelling, so never having checked 'abacus', we discover that it's from the Greek meaning 'a counting table'; the original abaci were created in the sand (Ref: Vocabulary.com).

Many children quickly come to realise that modern English words derive from languages across the world. This sometimes prompts questions such as –

How did words from other countries hundreds of years ago reach our country?

What does the word 'language' mean and where did the word come from?

When and why did humans begin using language in the first place? (An interesting book on this topic is 'Human Origins' as part of the New Scientist Instant Expert series – though even after reading it closely, we wouldn't say we had become an expert, instant or otherwise, of the subject. Indeed, the book is full of questions posed by scientists arising from their many different and often competing theories.)

Did language start in one place and spread, or did different people start using it separately in different places?

Do any animals have language?

What does a language actually need to consist of to be called a language?

Why do some words appear in the language and some words drop out?

What was the first language?

When this last question comes up, show the class an image of the so-called 'tree of language' (you might want to ask children why it's called a tree before showing them an illustration). Looking online, you'll find images readily available and the first thing children notice is how complex the language trees are, reflecting the way countries have interacted with each other over several millennia.

Another insight you can offer is that language is 'plastic', insofar that words change their meanings over time. For instance, the word 'nice' began as a negative Latin term meaning 'ignorant' or 'unaware', while Shakespeare used it in the sense of 'peculiar'. It has also meant 'exact' as in 'a nice shot'. Nowadays, it's a rather weak and watery word that means 'pleasant'. Many teachers advise young writers not to use it but to look for stronger adjectives. We've also found that many children are fascinated by listening to audio clips of Ancient Greek, Latin, Old English and so on. Although our current language has grown out of them, by and large our modern ear can make little or no sense of them.

It's also the case that words drop out of use and become obsolete while other words come into being. Words that have dropped out of use include croise, mussitate and conder (the spellchecker underlined all three in red!). As for new words, a rich source is to be found in terms related to the digital age – bot, bytes, internet, malware, spyware, teraflops and scores of others that simply didn't exist until recently. It turns out that the Oxford English Dictionary updates four times a year, adding hundreds of new words each time.

If this subject interests you, then books we've found useful are Isaac Asimov's 'Words of Science' (we could only find used copies online), 'History in English Words' by Owen Barfield, Melvyn Bragg's 'The Adventure of English' and Eilert Echwall's 'The Concise Oxford Dictionary of English Place-names' (again, we found only used copies available) and 'How Our Language Grew' by David Woodlander (this one's quite rare too). There are, though, many other books that are more readily available both used and new.

Activity: Using Proverbs

Proverbs (from the Latin 'putting forth the word') are a rich source of material for questioning, applying thinking skills and practising open-minded scepticism. Proverbs have been described as the insightful expression of a well-known truth imbued with ancestral wisdom, often passed down through the oral tradition.

Certainly when we were pupils, proverbs were 'taught' as part of the English syllabus. We say taught, but we have no recollection of our primary school teachers encouraging us to 'question, challenge and doubt' them; nor indeed, were we asked whether we agreed or disagreed with any given examples. (On a personal note, Steve still possesses his mid-1960s copy of 'The New First Aid in English' by Angus Maciver.

First published in 1938, this little gem of a book covers many aspects of English language and grammar, including proverbs, although here there's just a long list of them with no suggestion that they should be discussed and questioned: perhaps some creatively-minded teachers back then had the initiative to engage their children in this way. Incidentally, the book, revised and updated, is still in print.)

Even before looking at specific examples of proverbs, offer children the definition of a proverb and ask them to question it –

Do all proverbs fit the definition?

What is truth?

What is wisdom?

Are truth and wisdom the same? If not, how do they differ?

Thinking about 'ancestral' wisdom, does a proverb that might have been wise or true in the past apply to the modern day? Can you find examples that do and do not apply?

Are there any proverbs that were once wise or true in the past that are true or wise in a *different* way now?

Can any proverbs be changed to apply to the modern day?

With regard to particular proverbs, reinforce the question-challenge-doubt technique (or perhaps, rather, attitude). Also, ask children to look at the list of general questions to see if any apply. So, some examples –

It takes two to make a quarrel.

Are there any examples that refute this? For example, one nation attacking another without provocation (is 'quarrel' the best way to describe this?) or a habitual bully just looking to pick on a victim. Does one nation or person have to antagonise another actively for a quarrel to start? Or a person who's always angry and likes to pick a quarrel with someone who has a different opinion? Can two or more people who disagree do so without quarrelling – in other words, can they agree to disagree amicably?

A bad excuse is better than none at all.

Can excuses and lies be the same thing?

Is an excuse the same as a reason? If so, how are they similar? How might they be different?

What is meant by 'bad'?

What is meant by better? In what way? Who for?

What could be meant by a 'good' excuse? What examples can you think of? (The dog ate my homework, Miss – Steve used that one himself as a child. Didn't work.)

Is a bad excuse the same as a poor excuse? If not, how might they differ?

How is the word 'excuse' used here as a noun linked to 'excuse' as a verb, as in, 'Please excuse my untidy appearance'? Are they variations of the same root word?

New brooms sweep clean.

This is a metaphor: what does it mean in ordinary language?

What examples can we come up with of 'new ways' of doing things?

Can we think of any examples where change – sweeping away the old ways of doing things – was an improvement/not an improvement? (As we write this, the supermarket chain Booths has got rid of its automated checkouts and replaced them with human beings. Also, the plan to scrap ticket offices at railway stations has itself been scrapped, keeping the 'old way' of having manned ticket offices.)

The proverb is also a generalisation, suggesting that it is always or at least generally true. What other proverbs can you find that are a) metaphors, b) generalisations or c) both?

Practice makes perfect.

What does 'perfect' mean? (As a related issue, if perfect means 'cannot be bettered', how can someone who's not perfect recognise perfection?)

Can we think of any examples where the proverb is true?

Does the proverb contradict the idea of 'lifelong learning'; where perfection is never attained but where improvement is always a work in progress?

Do you personally regard anything as perfect?

Would you say that, for example, a circle is perfect? (Some interesting ideas crop up online when you key in 'Is a circle perfect?')

If you think that perfection exists anywhere, was it reached through practice?

Extend the activity by noting generalisations in books you read, programmes you watch etc. Present these to the class and ask pupils to discuss and challenge them. A couple we've recently come across are; 'All knowledge contains the promise of benefits' and 'True individuals are lonely.'

Challenge-focussed questions are likely to use the kinds of critical thinking we find in philosophical enquiries, such as –

What counts as knowledge?

How do you know 'all' knowledge?

What does the 'promise of benefits' actually mean? And what do you mean by 'benefits'?

If I discovered that my partner was betraying me in love, how might that be a benefit?

What other examples can you offer that support your assertion?

What do you mean by 'true'?

How do you define 'individuals'?

Does your statement imply individuals that are not, somehow, true?

Why are 'true' individuals lonely?

A teacher we know who worked in a children's day nursery would correct a member of her staff if they told a child that practice makes perfect: she would say, 'No – practice makes better.' How far do you or the children agree with this as a more accurate and reasonable idea? (Note the leading nature of this question!)

We think it's also the case that the proverb mentioned previously opens up the whole notion of 'natural talent', a rich area for discussion.

A heavy purse makes a light heart.

What does it mean to have a 'light heart'?

How could the proverb be rephrased to suit the digital age?

What if my purse was full of pennies that amounted to £1.43 – would that make for a light heart? And is 'heavy' a way of saying 'containing lots of money'?

The proverb is suggesting that the more money you have, the lighter your heart is; i.e. the more carefree and happier you are. Is that always true?

Can someone be poor materially but otherwise happy?

A traditional Japanese parable tells of a thief who entered the house of the Zen master Ryokan but found there was nothing in it worth stealing. Ryokan arrived home and caught him and out of kindness, offered the thief his clothes. When the thief had gone, Ryokan sat naked and felt sorry for the thief, wishing he could have given him the beautiful moon that was then shining in the sky. Ref: Parable 9 'The Moon Cannot be Stolen' in Paul Reps' 'Zen Flesh, Zen Bones.'

A Medley of Question-generating Activities

If you tell the children this parable, you might ask them the following questions –

Do you think that Ryokan is foolish, silly, mad? How would you describe him?

Do you think that anyone could have little or nothing in the way of possessions and yet value something like the beauty of the moon?

What does it mean to value something?

What is a 'value system': the collection of all the beliefs about what someone values?

Have you ever valued something that is worth nothing in monetary terms?

What is the relationship between 'value', in its different senses, and 'worth'?

Interestingly (and we think amusingly), a different proverb has it that 'what costs nothing is worth nothing.' Another activity would be to ask children to look through lists of proverbs to find contradictions. Do contradictory proverbs challenge the definition that proverbs are 'wise and true'? More subtly, can something be 'truer' than something else?

You can see that we are drifting here into philosophical realms and as such the proverb activity can be used as a precursor to introducing philosophy or as a warmup or lead-in to an enquiry, in this case about the concepts these questions have thrown up.

Here are some further proverbs to stimulate questions that you and the children can ask about them –

Live and let live.
Misfortunes never come singly.
Seeing is believing (ironic in the age of deepfakes!)
When in Rome, do as the Romans do.
The child is father to the man.

Another proverb-related exercise is to ask children to sum up the general point of view or attitude different proverbs express (this might be more appropriate for older pupils). So –

Time is money – materialistic.
There is a 'but' in everything – pessimistic.*
Where ignorance is bliss, it is foolish to be wise – naïve or even misguided.
Who knows most says least – big-headed.
Save me from my friends – cynical.

Feel free to disagree with us on any of these conclusions.

*Steve's first head of department often said that 'yesterday's optimist is today's realist, is tomorrow's pessimist' – one of the most deeply pessimistic and cynical views we think we've ever heard. Incidentally, a book that we leaf through often is Ambrose Bierce's 'The Enlarged Devil's Dictionary', which is full of the most cynical, incisive, sometimes infuriating and yet humorous definitions we've come across. For instance: 'Education – That which discloses to the wise and disguises from the foolish their lack of understanding.'

Activity: I Don't Know

Present children with a topic that you have yet to study; offer a few pieces of information about it as necessary, then ask children to come up with questions in advance. This not only reinforces the ethos that questioning is an expression of curiosity but gives you feedback as to what a given programme of study 'covers', and what else you will need to tell the children to answer their questions.

So, if you are about to study the Roman invasion of Britain, invite questions based on that topic. At a school Steve visited, children's questions included –

Is the word Roman linked to the city of Rome?
Why is Rome called Rome?
When did the Roman invasion of Britain happen?
Was the Roman invasion a completely bad thing?
When did the invasion end?
Why does one country invade another?
Did the people of Britain fight back? (And was it called Britain then?)
What did Roman soldiers look like?
Have other countries invaded or tried to invade Britain?
Could Britain be invaded in these modern times?

A linked activity is to ask the children if they have a hobby or area of interest and to tell the class what it is. Then invite classmates to come up with questions about that hobby (giving the questionee time to research answers if necessary).

For instance, one of Steve's interests is Astronomy. Some time ago a Year Five class, during an author visit, asked the following questions –

Why is astronomy so called?
Why are stars called stars?

Why is a galaxy called a galaxy? (There were lots of etymology-related questions. Steve didn't know the answer to this one. Subsequently, he found that it's from the Greek for 'milky', from *galakt,* meaning milk. Presumably this is related to the appearance of the Milky Way. We also suspect it's the inspiration for chocolate bars such as Galaxy and Milky Way. As a related activity, ask children to bring in examples of packaging from various grocery products or a list of their names and discuss/ speculate how those names came about.)

How does a telescope work?

What's the link between astronomy and astrology?

More searching questions were –

How did the universe begin?

How will the universe end?

Is there more than one universe?

Does life exist elsewhere in the universe (and do intelligent aliens exist)?

Is the universe an accident or did God make it?

Steve – I have to admit that I needed a lie down and two Paracetamols after wrangling with these questions. One well-informed child also asked what dark energy was, and it gave me a certain degree of comfort to say that nobody knows for sure at the moment, although for a thorough – and sometimes over my head – discussion of this try Brian Clegg's 'Dark Matter & Dark Energy: the hidden 95% of the universe.'

Activity: Marooned

As the title suggests, ask groups to imagine that they are marooned somewhere – in a crippled submarine on the sea bed, lost in the jungle with no GPS, in London with no money etc. Their task then is to work out a survival strategy by discussing and researching around the dangers, dilemmas and problems to be faced.

To help children, offer this guidance –

Give a detailed description of the situation.

What skills or personal attributes does the group possess (or would need) that would help them to get out of the situation?

What questions do you need to ask before you proceed?
What equipment would help you?
What decisions do you need to make at this point?

Ideas and conclusions can be presented in a number of ways as short stories or poems, fictional diary entries, letters or emails, pieces of scripted drama, improvised roleplay or artwork.

Activity: This Is the Answer – What Are the Questions?

The activity is self-explanatory. You or a child shows the class an answer and the rest of the children use it to generate questions. 'Answers' can be from any subject area and questions can either focus on that topic or range across a number of them. So, for instance, the 'answer' 1953 could generate mathematical questions or historical ones. Incidentally, if historical questions refer to fairly recent decades, a useful source of information is to be found in Robert Opie's series of so-called scrapbooks: Steve has the one for the 1950s that brings back memories of his early childhood. Opie's books are in large format, lavishly illustrated and contain some great period-related facts.

A similar activity uses a board game. The website twinkl.co.uk, for instance, offers a free download of two PDFs, one of a snakes and ladders board sprinkled with question marks, plus a set of question cards. Children play in small teams, following the usual snakes and ladders rules but picking up a card when landing on a question mark square. In our opinion, it's more fun if children create their own cards. Each appropriate question can move a player on a square, while one that doesn't fit means moving back a square.

Activity: Thinking Cards

Some years ago, a long-time friend of ours started up a small educational resources business – Thinking Child (sadly now defunct). One of the resources on offer was a pack of 'thinking cards', each card bearing a question designed to get children talking. Here are some of our favourites (reproduced with permission), together with a short commentary for each –

If you get paid for doing a job you love, can you still call it work?

Some children may simply look up a definition, such as 'work is an activity involving mental or physical effort done in order to achieve a purpose or result' (Oxford Languages). In this case, even if you loved doing a job, it would still be work. However, the notion of work often involves making an effort to do something that you don't love, such as homework – in Steve's case, it's gardening! In Tony's case, it's fitting Ring doorbells. Another response might be, 'I love working, full stop', in which case, end of argument we think.

If either computers or cars were going to vanish from the world, which would you prefer to see disappear and why?

Many years ago the science fiction writer Arthur C. Clarke said 'don't commute – communicate.' That vision is now eminently possible in many cases. The question also raises the point that whatever humans invent can bring benefits and dangers – perhaps children could list some related to both computers and cars. (As we write this, there are rumblings in the news about AI becoming ever more powerful, with warnings that artificial intelligence might run out of control.) The dangers of cars have long been recognised.

If you could take a pill to make you popular/more popular, would you do it?

For us, this is a particularly interesting question. The knee-jerk answer would be, yes who wouldn't? But some people might realise that the pill would result in a false or illusory popularity that had little or nothing to do with the person's inherent qualities and traits. In that case, whether to take it would be a question of conscience.

What things would you do if you were the last person on Earth?

This idea has been explored many times in science fiction. One of the most poignant was an episode of the original 'Twilight Zone' series – 'Time Enough to Last.' In a post-apocalyptic world, book-loving Henry Bemis, as far as we know the last person alive aims to indulge his love of reading: before the apocalypse, strict social control sanctioned the acquisition of knowledge through books (a theme also explored in Ray Bradbury's 'Fahrenheit 451', where 451°F is the flashpoint of paper as the totalitarian regime gathers up books to burn). Alone now but full of excitement, Bemis amasses the books he longs to read. As he reaches for the first one, his glasses fall off and being terribly short-sighted, he scrabbles around for his spectacles and accidentally smashes them, putting an end to his dream.

The character of Bemis was played by the excellent Burgess Meredith, and the episode (S1 Ep8) was first broadcast in November 1959. You can find out more by typing 'Time Enough to Last' into Wikipedia. We will also say that many of the episodes in Twilight Zone explore important themes very intelligently. If you are interested in SF at all, we thoroughly recommend the show.

Will you be a different person in five years' time?

Children with some experience of philosophy in school may well ask, 'What do you mean by different?' Certainly, many millions of our body cells will have been replaced after five years, while our experiences and thoughts continue to shape us throughout our lives. That said, there is also the notion of 'continuity of consciousness': although we age and may change our opinions and beliefs etc., there still seems to be an 'essential me' that remains constant. In that sense, there is some aspect of me that has not changed – the 'me of now' is essentially the same me as years ago, although I am older now and, we wonder, wiser.

The question reminds us of the well-known philosophical puzzle called The Ship of Theseus. Suppose that the Ancient Greek divine hero Theseus, proud of his ship, replaces parts of it periodically as they wear out. After some years, not a single element of the original ship remains, so is it the same ship?

Would you rather have all the money you need or be able to see into the future?

In one sense this question doesn't work because if you could see into the future you would know upcoming winning football pool results, race-horse winners and so on. However, it makes for an interesting activity for the class. . . Ask each of the children to think of a would-you-rather pairing. List these on the board and, as a class or with children in groups, get them to put some or all of the alternatives into an order of preference, backing up the choices with reasons.

If you could ask God three questions, what would they be?

Point out that even if some children don't believe in God, they can still reflect on the questions. One that comes up often is 'Why is there evil, pain and suffering in the world?' The standard answer is that these things need to exist in order for human beings to have free will; to be able to choose to be good or not and to believe in and love God or not. If God created everyone to be good and there was no evil, pain or suffering, then we'd be like programmed zombies unable to make up our own minds. With regard to the question of so-called 'natural evil'* such as earthquakes and hurricanes etc. the standard response is that they are an inevitable consequence of the way physical reality is set up: life, including human life, is only possible if the world and by extension the whole universe, 'works' in this way.

*We wonder if evil is the right word here.

This is an emotive issue and a complex one. The philosopher Peter Vardy has thoroughly explored the question in 'The Puzzle of Evil'.

A linked activity is to ask children to think of someone, fictional or real, alive or dead, that they would like to meet. What three questions would they ask that person? You might wish to prepare for this by running 'The Computer in the Box' game on page 70 and the 'Please Mr Einstein' activity on page 52.

What would happen if there were no clocks?

We've found that many children love playing with this idea, enjoying the supposed freedom that would result in not having to be in certain places at certain times. The question often brings out a mischievous streak – school timetables couldn't exist, while the whole notion of the school day would become much looser and more malleable. Could the notion of going to bed at a certain time cease to have any meaning? As a side issue, work with the class to show how deeply embedded the notion of time is in our language; playtime, teatime, bedtime, on time, early, later, before, after and many others. There's also the idea that clocks only measure time; that time would still pass even if all clocks vanished. But even so, would human civilisation unravel if we had no way of measuring time and correlating our actions? (Quick-witted children might point out that the cycle of day and night, the phases of the moon and the changing of the seasons are all natural ways of measuring time, out of which the earliest artificial methods of doing it, such as sundials, came about.)

If you are interested in the mystery that is time, a famous and grown-up book about it was written by the novelist and playwright J.B. Priestly. It's called 'Man and Time' and was edited by our dear late friend Douglas Hill. We also recommend H. G. Wells' wonderful short novel 'The Time Machine'. Suitable for older children, it's an allegory that explores the societal inequalities that existed in late-Victorian London.

Should we treat everyone exactly the same? Is it ever unfair to treat everyone equally?

Someone once said that equality in education isn't the same thing as giving the same education to everyone; that educational systems should address children's individual needs. Surely, all teachers understand and try to implement this ethos within the constraints that exist. On a more mundane level, would treating everyone equally mean that there would be no choice of school dinner or that we all had to wear the same style of clothes? Explore the question by looking at the notion of equality in different contexts.

If you lost your memory, would you become someone else?

We find this to be perhaps the scariest question of the selection we've presented. We remember reading the view some years ago that 'we are our memories'. The writer implies that we are *nothing more than* our memories and that these collectively give us our sense of self. It could also be argued that we need our powers of recall to think about the future or use our imaginations and that with no memories, we could have no forward-looking thoughts.

Children who are on the ball might suggest that the answer would differ depending on the extent to which memories were lost. If someone lost their memory of language, it would be more serious than losing their memory of what they did last week. The point also needs to be made that, depending on the degree to which memories were lost, horrifyingly a person might not be someone else but, rather, nobody at all.

The question also touches on the philosophical issue of what *is* the self. In a previous commentary to the question 'Will you be someone different in five years' time?' the notion of the continuity of consciousness cropped up, as mentioned earlier. There is a certain 'me-ness' that is continuous throughout our lives (barring tragic occurrences such as brain damage and dementia). When I am aware that I am aware, is that solely down to my store of memories? We have to admit that we haven't come to any conclusion. Some thinkers who believe that 'I' amounts to only one's memories also feel that the mind – out of which comes the 'I' – is only the product of brain activity; that a sense of self is just the product of the electrochemical activity of the brain. A different view is that somehow the brain acts as a transmitter for thoughts, in the same way that a TV serves to transmit programmes. Damage the TV and the transmission is affected, but because the information that makes up the programmes isn't generated by the TV, it still exists somewhere. This means that the mind isn't just the brain but needs the brain to express itself; this concept is called externalism. Also, this intimate relationship means that if the brain is damaged, the mind too will be affected. In the first of his 'Philosophy Files' books, philosopher Stephen Law devotes a chapter to the issue, as does Rupert Sheldrake in his 'The Science Delusion'.

Personally, we prefer the brain-as-transmitter idea, although hard-nosed materialists will argue that this is because it's more comforting since it suggests that perhaps the mind and sense of self can still exist after physical death. They may be right, though we want to be open-minded about it, preferring to leave the question open rather than closing off further reflection because of a dogmatic opinion.

Activity: The Computer in the Box

This is a kind of thought experiment for honing children's questioning skills. It works by asking the children to imagine that there is a super-intelligent computer inside a box. The rules for asking it questions are –

The computer will only accept questions that the children don't know the answers to.
It will only answer questions that are absolutely clear and unambiguous.
Because its battery power is low, it can only answer three questions posed by the class.

Obviously, the first part of the activity consists of children coming up with questions that they regard as important. We daresay there will be more than three, so discussion will be needed to whittle down to the three questions that everyone can agree are important. It would also be useful for children to give their reasons as to why the questions are significant.

The next step is to check the shortlist of questions for vagueness or ambiguity. For example, if we ask, 'What should we do about poverty in this country?' then we can query it – Who does 'we' refer to? What does 'should' mean? How do we define poverty?

You might want to prepare children for this stage by introducing or revisiting the idea of ambiguity. Show them questions such as –

The chicken is ready to eat – is a live chicken about to consume food or has a chicken been cooked and is now ready to be eaten?

He was carrying a light box – was he carrying a box that doesn't weigh much or a box that can become illuminated?

Half of his money, which amounted to a million pounds, was left to three different charities – did the money amount to a million pounds or half a million pounds?

The teacher only glanced at Steve's essay – was Steve's the only essay the teacher looked at, or did the teacher give Steve's essay just a brief look?

The school was built roughly around 1953 – was the school built some time around 1953, or was it shoddily (roughly) built in 1953?

Incidentally, one of the most amusing ambiguous sentences we've come across was supposedly by a botanist called Moses Hadas, who replied to the gift of a book by writing to the author, 'Thank you for sending me a copy of your book. I shall waste no time reading it.'

The computer in the box game helps to prepare children for the kinds of thinking they need to do during a philosophical enquiry and, indeed, can help to generate a stock of questions for future discussions. We'll look more closely at this later, but for now we'll say that the most enjoyable enquiries are based on questions that the children feel are important to them and that during a session, they need to be clear about what they mean.

4 Questions and Creative Writing

The writer Douglas Hill (a close friend of ours who sadly passed away in 2007) once said that the whole of science fiction is predicated on the question 'what if'. By extension, most ideas in fiction begin in the same way. After that first inspiration, a writer lets the story unfold by asking scores or even hundreds of further questions, sometimes explicitly, but certainly at a subconscious level – the proof of this being when insights that work well in a story pop 'out of the blue' fully formed. At a basic level, writing is about asking questions, making decisions and arriving at answers or conclusions that drive the work forward, most satisfyingly in a state of flow. Perhaps all branches of art are like this.

However, questioning can also be used in many other ways to help children to not only develop plots, characters and settings but to help young writers move on if they feel they've 'got stuck' during the writing itself.

Activity: The Counter-flip Game

At its most basic, the activity consists of asking closed questions and flipping a two-colour counter to obtain a yes or no answer. The basic rules are –

An answer must be accepted once the counter has been flipped.

Questions must be relevant, not silly or inappropriate.

Questions must not be contradictory. If the counter tells us that a scene takes place at night, we cannot then ask subsequently if the same scene takes place in the daytime.

Children can start anywhere and from nothing. You might prompt the class by asking an initial question – 'Let's invent a character. Is it

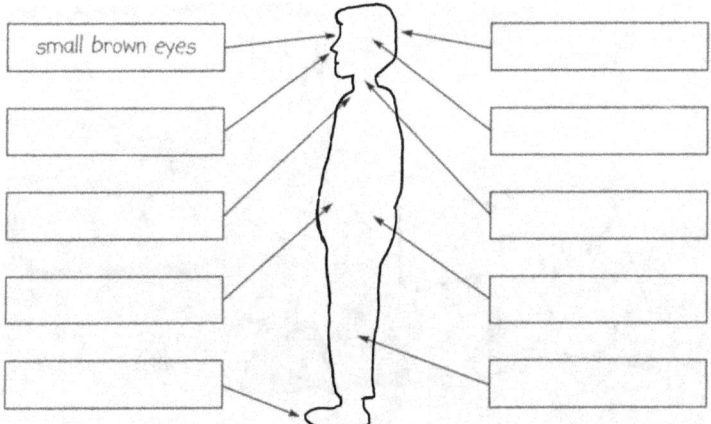

Figure 4.1 Children are asked to look at different parts of a character they are creating and think of two adjectives to help describe a body part, such as small brown eyes.

a child?' 'Will our story be set, or begin, in a city?' Take the activity further by asking for short descriptive phrases that demand a choice, so think of a character – hair – long or short? Straight or curly? Fair or dark? Children can either decide for themselves or flip a counter to select an answer. If they come up with more than two options, do two counter flips – Is the hair either fair or black? If yes, flip to choose between the two. If no, flip to select one of the other options.

This activity can quickly create a 'character thumbnail' that can be expanded as the story evolves, as in Figure 4.1.

Extend the activity by asking questions around the adjective-adjective-noun choices to add more detail to the character. So, if we learn that a character has small brown eyes, related questions might be – 'Does the character wear glasses? If yes, are the glasses for reading and close work? Does the character like reading? What kinds of fiction/non-fiction does the character like to read?' And so on.

Advise children to keep questions general in the early stages. If the first question from a child is 'Is this a Fantasy story?' and the answer is yes, then the whole class is 'locked' into that genre and would be forced to ask further fantasy-related questions to develop the storyline. Once a basic scenario becomes clear however, children can then work in small groups, pairs, or individually within their own preferred genres.

Another way of kick-starting the questioning is to use a picture, as in Figure 4.2, preferably one that's slightly ambiguous so that one of a number of things could be happening. We also like to use black and white images so that children can imagine the colours that might be

74 *Question Quest for Ages 8–14*

Figure 4.2 This image is ambiguous: various things could be going on. Children are encouraged to ask questions and flip the two-colour counter to build up an impression of what might be happening.

there before going on to imagine sounds and then in their imaginations to go 'into' the picture to imagine smells and textures and even move beyond the frame of what the image actually shows.

Some children find that even after a relatively small number of questions have been asked, the rest of the story appears magically in their minds (more subconscious assimilation). In that case, you might let those children go off to do their writing while you work with the rest of the class on the game.

Occasionally, even after running the game, some children begin writing enthusiastically but then run out of steam or find that the story isn't working as well as they thought it would. In such cases, encouraging them to pause and do some counter-flips around what might happen next will usually give them a sense of direction and get them writing again. Using a narrative line (page 53) can also help to organise ideas and work out the rest of the plot. As children become more confident and experienced creative writers, you can suggest that they would perhaps think of more than one way in which their story might develop – see 'Pluralising' on page 28.

A variation of the activity is to show the class the title of a story or allow children to pick or make up their own and use that as a starting point for counter-flip questions. Or you might show the class the back-cover blurb of a published story that they haven't read or use a synopsis as the basis for their own counter-flip adventure.

Apart from generating ideas, the game is useful because it takes away children's anxiety about getting answers wrong: they realise that the counter is responsible for the answers while understanding the importance of asking relevant, story-building questions. Also, over time, many children will come to ask increasingly incisive questions that develop the story more quickly and effectively.

The counter-flip game is actually more sophisticated than this. We've explained it much more fully in 'Visualising Literacy and How To Teach It.'

Activity: Story Strips

Plots can also be built up by using simple images arranged linearly, as in Figure 4.3 –

Figure 4.3 This Figure asks children to take three simple images and link them as the basis for a simple narrative.

Children are likely to begin weaving the images into the start of a narrative quickly and naturally, especially if you remind the class that there is no single right answer to the relationship between the pictures. So, as in Figure 4.4, we might get –

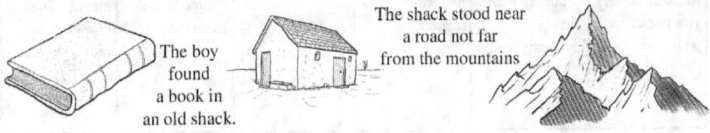

Figure 4.4 Once children have formed an initial link between the images, as exemplified in Figure 4.3, they are asked to write up the links using simple sentences to create a rudimentary storyline.

An entire narrative can be created this way, or children can take just this section and begin asking the six 'big important questions'; where, when, what, who, why, how? At some point, the linkages can be incorporated into a formally written story, as in Figure 4.5.

A similar activity is the 'filmstrip technique' as in Figure 4.6. Here, children take a broader brush approach and build a plot prompted by a more detailed picture. Increase the number of ideas by giving different groups 'filmstrips' with the picture placed in different cells.

76 Question Quest for Ages 8–14

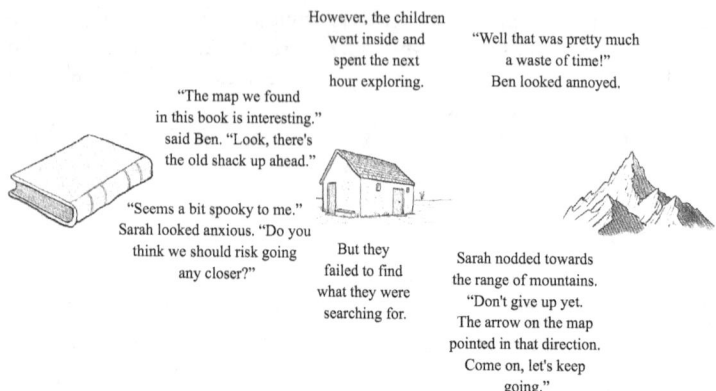

Figure 4.5 Children are now encouraged to expand on their ideas by composing full sentences in story form, using the linked images as prompts.

Figure 4.6 This image reinforces the idea of a linear narrative by placing a picture along a line of otherwise blank cells.

Activity: Story Strings

These consist of a variety of beads threaded on a string to mirror the linear structure of simple narratives. They are best used on a one-to-one basis, with the child suggesting possible scenarios as she handles her way along the string. Alternatively, two children can work together, passing the string back and forth to one another and discussing the beads and how they might form the basis of a narrative or 'seed story' that can be

Questions and Creative Writing 77

developed further subsequently. The beads can be in the shape of actual objects or be more abstract (see also thinking about 'Ambiguous Shapes' on page 33). Size, shape and colour can all act as clues as to how the beads might relate to an evolving narrative. Figure 4.7 is a simple example.

The activity can be made more complex by using more beads, as Figure 4.8a-c demonstrates. Of course, you'll appreciate that when children handle story strings, their experience is all the richer because of the size, shape, colour and texture of the beads as well as the sounds they make; any or all of these aspects of the strings might spark off new ideas.

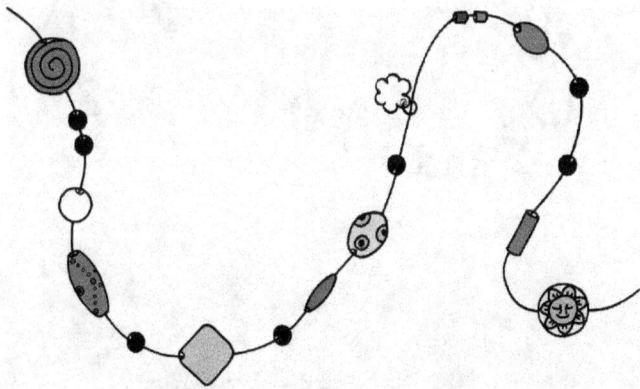

Figure 4.7 The illustration shows beads on a string and is an extension of the linear narrative concept highlighted in the previous few figures.

Figure 4.8 These Figures show story strings of increasing complexity.

78 Question Quest for Ages 8–14

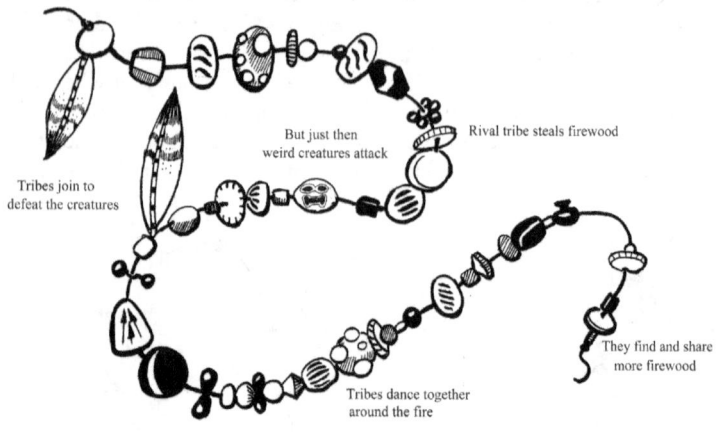

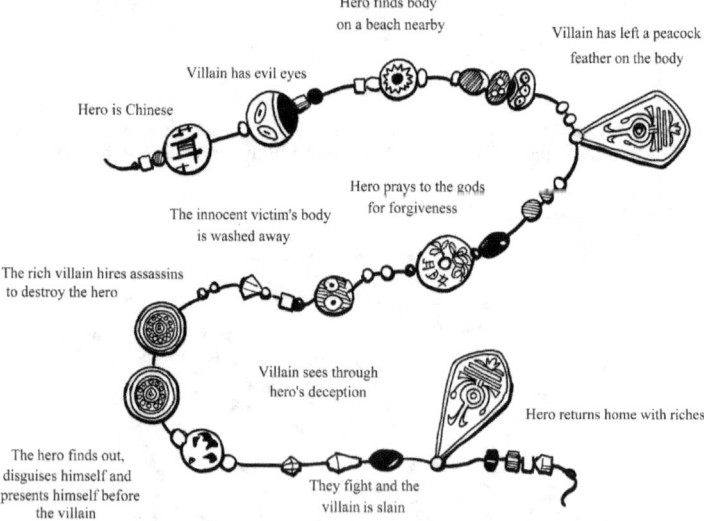

Figure 4.8 (Continued)

The story string examples beg many questions: remember that these narratives were created spontaneously, with ideas just popping into the children's minds. There is a certain degree of logic attached to them, but you can take the activity further by inviting children to ask questions about the plot. So, with regard to the story string in Figure 4.8a, we might ask –

Why did Monkey want to make a wish?

What did Monkey wish for?

In what way is the ball magic?

Is Tinkerbell's arrival linked to the wish or the ball or is it just a coincidence?

Why did Tinkerbell give Monkey a balloon?

What happened to Monkey after he floated away? In other words, how might we continue the story (perhaps by using a selection of loose beads as suggested further on)?

Tip: Have a supply of loose beads to hand, either in a bag and/or spread out on the table. To answer a question, a child can either do a lucky dip into the bag, anticipating that the randomly chosen bead will spark an idea, or select from the beads on the table, or use both as you tackle the list of questions. Either way, the more a bead sparks an idea or answer, the more confident the child will become in her own creative abilities. A variation of the activity is to use only loose beads – i.e. not ones strung on twine – and ask children to create lines of beads as they discuss possible plots. The advantage of this is, of course, that children can add further beads anywhere into the line as more ideas come along or remove beads if, after discussion, they don't seem to take the story anywhere.

The story of 'The Monkey's Wish' was created by a seven-year-old. Notice how it has an almost surreal fairy tale quality to it: in fairy tales, the strangest and most fantastical things happen and often have the weird and symbolic nature of dreams (we explore this idea further in 'Understanding the World Through Narrative'). Older children will tend to create more rational and logical plots, but encouraging young children to ask questions around fairy-tale-like story string narratives will help to develop their rational thinking abilities.

Tip: We wouldn't advise you to prompt other children to put questions to the creators of story string tales if they aren't very confident, as they may feel pressured and even embarrassed if they can't come up with ready answers. However, you might want to present the story creators with other children's answers to the questions they've considered and ask the story string authors what they think about them.

Admittedly, it takes time and effort to source the beads and thread them (although children might enjoy creating story strings for themselves). If you let children do this, you'll notice that pairs or small groups working together will make up at least one story as they decide on the order of the beads. And of course, when the story strings are made, they form a permanent resource that can be used with future classes.

Once a child or pair has come up with a story, invite them to turn the story string around so that the end becomes the beginning of a different story.

Activity: Similarities and Differences

Different authors will describe people, places and events in different ways depending on many factors, such as the form the writing takes – poetry or prose, for example – or the emotional impact the writer aims to achieve, as well as authors' varying styles. The simplest way to run this activity is to show the class a picture of a person, object, etc. and ask children to write a brief description and then compare the ways in which it's been done. You can increase the challenge by inviting children to pick up a 'chance card' if they wish – these give a prompt to suggest the direction the writing will take. So, 'this person is a criminal' 'this person is a film star' and so on. Of course, children can create their own prompts on scraps of paper. Put them in an envelope to be picked out at random.

A more challenging activity amounts almost to literary criticism, where you (or the children as a research task) pick an object and find examples in literature that are then compared and contrasted. As children become more familiar with doing this, their critical thinking skills will be sharpened and many are likely to feel increasingly confident to express their observations. For older pupils, a useful source of information can be found at www.descriptionari.com/, although the varying descriptions we've come across there have been penned by the same author, so you might also try Quora.com, https://www/writerswrite.co.za/, www.countryliving.com/ and www.goodreads.com

More on characters:

Activity: Character Thumbnails

We first came across these on page 73. Take the activity further by asking children to write a brief description of their counter-flip character using full sentences. They can also leave some details blank for classmates to fill in, as in Figure 4.9.

Questions and Creative Writing 81

Name: Philippa Stephens. **Age:** 11 years. **Description:** tall, dark hair, blue eyes, gentle face. She is usually in a good mood, but can have a terrible temper if things don't go her way. She has one brother, Robert, 12, and a cat called Mog. She loves him to bits. **Add further information:**	**Name:** Paula Samra. **Age:** .... **Description:** Long fair hair, brown eyes. Paula left school when she was .... and now works as a .... She is usually very .... and .... Her special claim to fame is .... **Add further information:**
Name: Jason Marsden. **Age:** 12. **Description:** .... Jason comes from a .... family. His hobbies are .... And especially .... **Add one more fact:**	**Name:** Ben Leech. **Age:** .... **Description:** .... At .... he went to .... Where he .... And ....

Figure 4.9 This image extends the idea of character development shown in Figure 4.1. by asking children to use full descriptive sentences instead of the simpler adjective-adjective-noun pattern.

You'll see that the technique is versatile: you can decide what and how much information you want children to supply. Also, children can create their own character thumbnails by drawing people or using pictures from magazines, etc. Ask children to stick their pictures onto lined A6 file cards and fill in some character details, as in Figure 4.9, for classmates to complete. If you want the cards to be a permanent resource, photocopy them for children to write on.

Linked activities include inviting children to choose two or more thumbnails at random and discuss what these people might say to each other in a given situation; photocopy just the image of a character, glue it in the middle of a large sheet of paper and ask small groups to brainstorm an association web around that person. Children can also create character thumbnails based on stories they've read.

Activity: Add-a-bit

This amounts to a collective and collaborative way of creating characters. The idea is to write a brief opening sentence about a character on a sheet of paper. The paper is then passed on from child to child, with each child adding a further detail. So, 'Ben is quite shy – He has one person he calls his best friend – Ben has dark hair – He is young-looking for his age – He is 11 – He loves reading books . . .' And so on. Alternatively, ask children to frame their add-on bits as questions, so 'How confident is Ben?' 'Does Ben have a best friend?' 'How old is Ben?' and 'What does Ben most enjoy doing?'

Whether add-ons are written as statements or questions, children will be progressively challenged to keep what they write consistent with an increasing amount of information.

Once the paper has done the rounds of the class, Ben, in this case, should be quite a richly developed character, though check for contradictions and 'silly' details (Ben has green skin and wings and he can fly). That said, such fantastical details can be used creatively by asking the originator to come up with a plausible reason *why* Ben should have these qualities and how they could be used in a story or poem. If other children are persuaded, then you can let the detail pass.

A number of add-a-bit sheets can be circulating around the class at any one time; that way, children will not get bored waiting for their turn and will also have to think flexibly as different characters are passed to them.

An extension of the activity is to create a set of 'situation cards' and ask children, once characters have been created, how they would react in a randomly chosen situation. This helps children to understand and build logical consistency in their writing. So, if Ben and his best friend were being bullied at school, although Ben might feel intimidated and frightened, he might stand up to the bully to help protect his friend. And if an add-a-bit sheet had been done for the friend, children would have greater insight into how he-or-she and Ben might react in the given situation. Of course, situation cards can also be created by the children and form a permanent resource for future use.

Activity: Character Wheel

If children want to think more deeply about characters, one way of accumulating details is to use a character wheel, Figure 4.10, where each segment reflects the importance or prominence of different traits in a given character's life.

Questions and Creative Writing 83

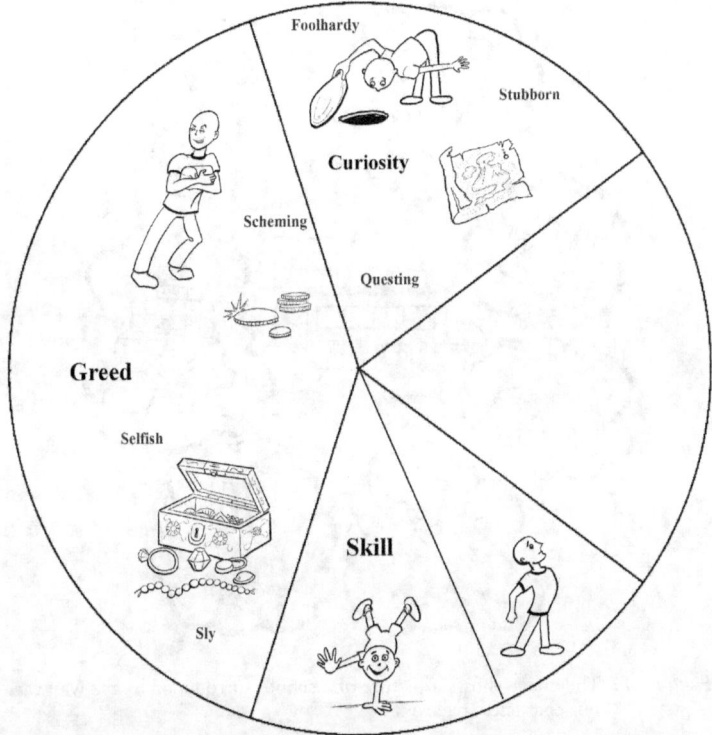

Figure 4.10 This activity goes beyond physical description and asks children to think about the personalities of characters they might choose to use in a story.

Character wheels can be built up over time, especially if a child uses the same character across a number of stories.

Activity: Viewpoints

This activity calls on children to interpret how characters feel about the same object, place or another person while developing children's ability to think metaphorically. The example in Figure 4.11 shows how a group of friends regard their local school.

Ask children to interpret how characters A-G view their school. Take it further by encouraging children to discuss what any character's viewpoint says about that person. So the viewpoint of character

Figure 4.11 The image shows a picture of a school surrounded by the way various characters regard it.

A might suggest that he is competitive and takes pride in his sporting achievements.

If appropriate, explain that we all see the world through the 'filters' of our own previous experiences, so if someone was bullied at school, he might see it as a dangerous labyrinth, or if a child has just moved up from primary school she might see her new secondary school as huge and confusing.

Steve – On a personal note, some years ago, I visited the village in South Wales where I spent my childhood 50 years after our family moved away. It all seemed so small and cramped! The walk to the shops as a child seemed to take ages, whereas now, as an adult, it was just a couple of hundred yards. The world can certainly look different as we grow up.

Activity: Settings

Descriptions of settings can also be created using counter flips, although some children will look at a suggested location for a story and immediately imagine a richly detailed scenario. Another activity is to get the

Questions and Creative Writing

Locked up funfair	Country lane	Seashore	Ancient mansion	Canal towpath	Old railway line
Night bus/ train	Deserted warehouse	Stone circle	Museum at night	Remote hills	Ordinary house
Boarded up flats	Old castle	Strange village	Library	Shopping mall	Woodland path
A park	Abandoned church	Graveyard	River	Foggy street	Waste ground
Tumbledown house	Old fashioned hotel	Allotments	Alley	Accident blackspot	Junkyard
Empty school	Industrial estate	Overgrown garden	Lonely road	Lake	Haunted inn

Figure 4.12 Settings are as important in story-making as characters. This Figure offers a selection of genre-related settings.

class to brainstorm settings; having chosen a theme or genre, place them in a 6x6 grid and either use dice rolls to choose one at random or select through discussion/decision making. Figure 4.12 is specific to Fantasy or Horror stories.

Activity: Questioning the Answers

Take a simple image such as Figure 4.13 –

Figure 4.13 A simple image invites children to ask questions about it – in this case, how did a character find the book, what is the book about, etc.

Then invite children to ask questions about it, without at this stage trying to come up with any answers –

Where did the book come from?
How is it important or unusual?

Why might the book have a lock on it?
Where is the key?
Why would one or more of the characters in the story be interested in it?

Now ask the children to suggest possible answers. These can be general or genre-specific. Use brainstorming if you wish –

Where did the book come from?
Our main character bought it from a second-hand bookshop.
It was left to one of the characters in their great uncle's will.
Some kids found it in the woods.

It appeared mysteriously on the doorstep one day.

Now invite children to ask questions about each of these possibilities –

- Why was the character in the bookshop interested in that particular book?
- Why did the great uncle leave the book to that particular relative?
- Who left the book in the woods and why?
- What were the children doing in the woods in the first place?
- Why would someone leave the book anonymously at that address?

You can see where this is going... Take each of these questions in turn and ask children to suggest possible answers. Repeat the questioning-the-answers process as many times as necessary. The usefulness of the activity is that it generates a lot of 'raw material' that can evolve into a number of plots rather than just one (see 'Pluralising' on page 28). Because each question generates a number of answers, and vice versa, each child can pick his own preferred route into a story and, if he wishes, split off from the main group to continue exploring individually. The wealth of questions and answers also serves as a resource for further story-writing sessions.

Activity: First Lines, Last Lines

Offer the class a selection of opening lines and their corresponding last lines from some stories and ask the children to discuss what might happen in between. They can use the counter-flip game if they wish to guide their thinking.

'When we hung around up the lane one of our favourite games was to put a bunch of empty tin cans in a line on top of the wall. Then we'd all stand in a row about 12 feet away, each of us armed with a small handful of stones. In turns, we'd throw a stone and if we knocked a can off the wall, we had another go, but had to take a step back. If we missed a can, the next kid in line had a go. / So that's how Anna Williams joined our group.'

'The skeleton tripped over Dracula's polished shoe and went sprawling on the grass. With a shriek of delight, the vampire swirled up his cloak, turned and ran away through the trees. Eleanor Trent burst into a fit of giggles, but the skeleton – actually Tommy Hyatt, who lived on Arkham Road – groaned and winced and held his aching back as he scrambled to his feet. / Diana shrugged and chuckled, nodded and smiled. She draped her good hand around Eleanor's shoulder like old pals as they walked home.'

'The posters had gone up a week ago, in shop windows and on telegraph poles all over the small rural town on Oakhills – 'Arturo Fellini presents – The Greatest Travelling Fairground in the Nation!'/ You've given me more than you'll ever know, Nick Scace, Natalie thought. Not just a good time and not just a fortnight I'll never forget. But new dreams.'

Activity: Story Grids

Showing the class a picture grid, such as the example in Figure 4.14, allows children to have ideas in a number of ways. Because all of the pictures are constantly visible, children will naturally tend to link two or more to create new ideas – The dragon attacked the castle/The king found a magic mirror that can look into the future/The hooded figure entered the maze looking for treasure/The owl saw a thief stealing a bag of money. And so on. The creative linking process can be done more systematically by using dice rolls. Two rolls of a die – along the corridor and up the stairs – pinpoint one of the images. Do this twice and link the two images in a sentence; so 5/6 is a gate and 6/6 is the dragon – You need to speak some magic words to pass through the gate and enter the dragon's kingdom. Children will come up with a range of scenarios using those same images.

The next step is to encourage the children to ask questions about the chosen sentence –

- How do you find the magic words to open the gate?
- Where is the gate?
- Does the character already know about the gate? If not, how do they find out?
- Why does our character need to meet with the dragon?

88 Question Quest for Ages 8–14

Figure 4.14 The picture shows a 6x6 grid of images that children can use to develop their story-making abilities.

- Is the dragon evil or good?
- Is our character evil or good?

Children can either create answers for themselves or use the 'Counter-flip' technique (page 72) to obtain answers. The use of both dice and the counter brings randomness into the activity by what we like to call 'taking the mind by surprise'. Instead of *trying* to have ideas, which can be frustrating and fruitless, ideas tend to come spontaneously as the two images are connected.

The next step is to pick one of the questions and roll the dice twice more to find a third image, which will either answer the question or give a clue to the answer. So, for instance, to find out why the character needs to meet the dragon, roll twice – 2/1 the hooded figure –

The hooded figure has put a spell on the princess and only the dragon can break it.
The dragon has been imprisoned by the hooded figure and the king wants to free him.
The dragon is fading out of existence and the hooded figure knows how to prevent this.

An evil sorcerer has turned the hooded figure into a dragon and the king wants to use the book of spells to free him.

Children can now ask questions about the ideas they've created –

- Why did the hooded figure put a spell on the princess?
- Why did the hooded figure choose the princess in particular?
- Why did the hooded figure imprison the dragon?
- What happened to cause the dragon to begin fading out of existence?
- Why did the sorcerer turn the hooded figure into a dragon – and why a dragon?
- How does the king obtain the book of spells?

Further dice rolls to select other images will often suggest answers to these questions, or they might be reached through discussion. Again, the usefulness of the technique lies in the fact that children won't find themselves struggling to have ideas: ideas will tend to pop up 'out of the blue' due to the children's natural creativity and the fact that as soon as they are shown the grid they will be subconsciously assimilating and linking the images, allowing ideas to appear without effort. Steve has used story grids for many years in his creative writing workshops and has found time and again that children's confidence improves when they realise that they can make up stories quite effortlessly. And once children have learned how the grids work, many are keen to create their own by drawing pictures, using clippings from comics, or downloading images from the internet. A great story-grid project, in our opinion, is to get the whole class to contribute to a giant story grid put up on a display board. Children from other classes can be invited in to learn how story grids work and then create their own plots. Also, using genre-specific grids helps children to become familiar with the motifs and conventions of different genres, including the constituent features of a story and how they are used.

Note: You can find further examples of story grids in 'Developing Thinking Skills Through Creative Writing' (Bowkett & Hitchman, 2020).

Activity: Strength of Reasons Revisited

As we've seen, many such questions can have a number of answers that will be more or less likely or believable. Robust reasons help to establish the believability of a story, while statements made during a philosophical enquiry have more impact if they have been reasoned out (see page 9). Pose the question, 'Why would aliens invade Earth?' show the class these possible reasons and ask children to evaluate their 'strength' on a 1–6 scale, with one being a weak reason and six being a robust reason. (Alternatively, base a strength-of-reasons question on ideas children have come up with based on a story grid.)

Why would aliens invade the Earth?

They are mad.

Their home world is about to be destroyed by their sun going nova. (How many children will ask what a nova is, we wonder?)

They got bored and wanted something to do.

They need Earth's natural resources to expand their technology.

Earth is a stepping stone to building a galactic empire.

An ancient, technologically sophisticated and extinct race from Earth invaded their planet long ago and this is the aliens' revenge.

The alien race is dying and needs to implant their minds into human bodies.

Note that you can also use these reasons with the 'Questioning the Answers' technique, as explained on page 85.

Activity: Back to the Grids

Another use of the grids is to use images literally or metaphorically to create short pieces of writing around a given theme. Poems work well – here's one that was created by a class around the theme of 'Peace' using Figure 4.14 on page 88.

> Peace means the sword will not fall.
> The raging fires will stop.
> Peace means we hear the owl's soft call
> And the leaves will gently drop.
>
> Peace means the dragon falls asleep
> And calms its flames;
> The witch ends her spells
> And the maze its secrets keep.

This kind of activity helps children to explore and more closely define abstract concepts, which serve as a useful precursor to setting up a philosophy session.

As children become more familiar with the benefits of using story grids, they may well want to create some of their own, perhaps based on

Questions and Creative Writing

favourite stories or entirely from scratch. These can form a permanent resource bank for subsequent groups.

Activity: Story Dice

You may be familiar with story dice in the form of sets of dice that have images printed on them. As we write this, Steve has on his desk a set of ghost story dice (that come in a glow-in-the-dark box!) produced by Laurence King Publishing and a set of 'Rory's Story Cubes' (www.storycubes.com/en/). Both sets invite children to roll the dice and link as many of the images as possible in a narrative, or what we might call a 'proto-narrative', as the stories will be refined through further thought. Fewer dice can be rolled to make the activity easier.

We want to open up the idea of using dice to create stories – other than by using them with story grids, as we've explained earlier. Take a number of differently coloured dice and use these in conjunction with a grid, as shown in Figure 4.15.

You'll see that we've kept this grid 'genre neutral' although children can choose particular genres that appeal to them and even motifs from particular stories that they've enjoyed. The basic idea is to roll a number of the coloured dice and then check the motifs in the cells corresponding to the numbers that come up. So if the purple die rolls 3, we come up with 'artefact'. If we roll a 5 with the orange die, we get 'landscape' and so on, using as many of the dice as the children feel comfortable with.

The activity can also be combined with the counter flip game and the questions-answers-further-questions technique explained earlier. The random nature of using dice rolls prompts the spontaneous appearance of ideas, while counter flips and questioning are more focussed and systematic.

	Purple	Orange	Green	Red	Yellow	White	Blue	Black
1	Sidekick	Value	Dark	Join	Travel	Share	Weather	Value
2	Ancient	Illusion	Betrayal	Leave	Barrier	Live	Catch	Abandon
3	Artefact	Gate	Hidden	Move	Time	Revealed	Delay	Vehicle
4	Book	Lie	Space	Taken	Miss	Group	Round	Trust
5	Dream	Landscape	Cause	Message	Secret	Edge	Gather	Release
6	Territory	Plan	Meeting	Return	List	Locate	Avoid	Trick

Figure 4.15 The Figure is a template for using coloured dice rolls to increase the sophistication of the random-choice technique in story-making.

5 More Challenging Activities

Activity: Grid Work

We've already looked at how to use a 6x6 grid of ambiguous shapes to stimulate creative thinking focussed on a 'real world problem'. A more challenging use of the grids is to present the class with two grids and have children pick one or two items from each and link them in a way that develops a story, moves closer to resolving a problem, etc. in Figure 5.1 and 5.2 are two sample grids, but you and/or the children may want to create your own.

Using the grids, roll dice to find the coordinates of two images on the picture grid and link them in a sentence and then ask children (without dice rolls if you wish) to pick two concepts from the word grid that are linked in some way. Then move on to one of the tasks outlined in the previous paragraph.

A variation of the activity, using only the word grid, is to ask children to pick two concepts that are linked in some way, such as Mind and Thought. Discuss what some of the words mean. If children are struggling with definitions, suggest they do some research rather than just giving them the answer (to the extent that answers are possible. How might we define Reality, for instance?).

Alternatively, taking one or more of the words in the grid, frame questions using them as a focus. For example –

The poet John Keats said, 'Beauty is truth, truth (is) beauty.' What might he have meant? If someone has cosmetic surgery to make themselves look more beautiful, is beauty still truth in that case?

The Victorian writer Margaret Wolfe Hungerford supposedly said that 'Beauty is in the eye of the beholder.' What might she have meant by that? A friend of Steve's keeps snakes and lizards as pets and thinks that they are beautiful. He has a phobia about snakes and so, while Steve can appreciate that some are beautifully coloured, he could

More Challenging Activities   93

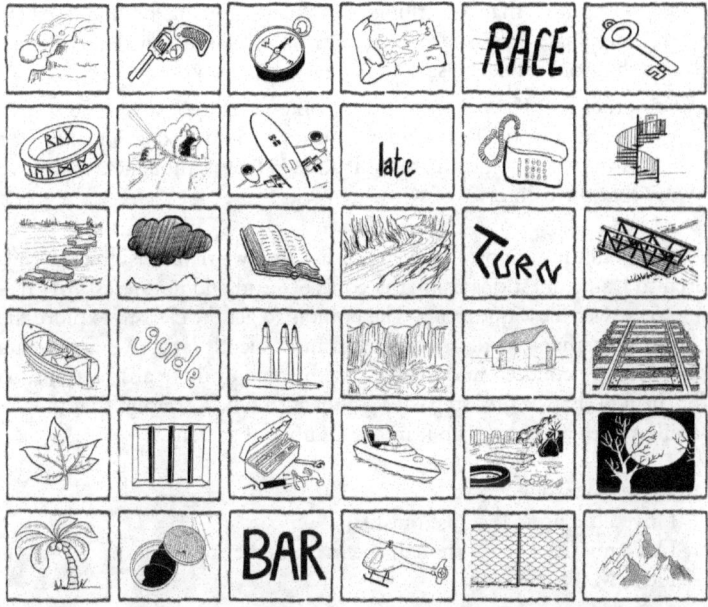

Figure 5.1 6x6 story grids can focus on specific genres. This one shows the kinds of ideas that would feature in an action-adventure story.

Beauty	Myth	Trust	Conscience	Humanity	Love
Nature	Knowledge	Mind	Life	Choice	Wisdom
Thought	Cause	Friendship	Truth	Reason	Duty
Memory	Peace	Creativity	Justice	Loyalty	Self
Rights	Happiness	Existence	Judgement	Mercy	Reality
Community	Intelligence	Conflict	Facts	Time	Evil

Figure 5.2 This figure develops children's thinking about abstract concepts and how they can be used in narratives.

never feel that they are beautiful in the same way as his friend does. How do you think Steve's and his friend's definitions of the beauty of the snakes might differ?

What does it mean to be human? What other concepts in the grid contribute to what it means to be human? Are there concepts that can also apply to animals – these too can be framed as questions. . .

Steve thinks his cat Leo loves him. Do you think that cats and dogs can love their owners? If you do, how might Leo's love be different from Steve's love for his wife?

How do we know that something exists? Can thoughts be said to exist? If something exists, is it real? For example, a fantasy novel exists, but can the story it tells be said to be real in any way?

Steve's other cat, Kitty, passed away some years ago, so she no longer exists. But he still has vivid memories of and strong affection for Kitty. In that sense, the cat is still alive in Steve's thoughts, so can we say that the memories of Kitty are real?

At this point, it's important to emphasise that we're just asking the children to frame questions using the concepts grid and not necessarily trying to answer these questions. The point is to get the class to explore the concepts, perhaps to discuss them in more depth later. We appreciate that younger children may struggle with some of these abstractions, so for them perhaps a first step is to get them to take a concept that they're familiar with and just drop it into a number of sentences –

I love macaroni cheese.
I loved the book I've just finished.
I love my sister (even though she irritates me sometimes).
I love Maths.

And so on. The next step would be to talk about how the idea of love is different in these examples, perhaps by looking at synonyms (which might, on reflection, turn out not to be precisely synonymous).

Again, using concepts that the children understand do any appear in stories – fictional or factual – that the children know about? For instance, the hero in many stories fights for the right of people to be free and left in peace. What then do we mean by 'right' in this case?

Another angle is to look up the origin of some of the concept words, which might spark further questions –

Beauty – from Latin meaning pretty, handsome, charming, pleasant, fine; linked also to the Latin terms for good and virtuous. And, of course, these other terms can be researched for their origins. They can also be used to generate further questions –

In what way is someone who's charming also beautiful? Can a person be charming but not beautiful and vice versa? Are a pretty person and a handsome person beautiful in the same way?

If someone is good and virtuous but not pretty or handsome, can we say that they are beautiful 'on the inside' or that that aspect of their character is beautiful?

In what sense is 'fine' linked to being beautiful? We might describe an antique vase as a fine piece of work, though you might think it's beautiful and we might think it's ugly. Is that an example of beauty being in the eye of the beholder? If a hundred people think the vase is beautiful and we think it's ugly, can we say objectively or definitely that the vase is beautiful? If a ceramics expert says the vase is beautiful, does that make it beautiful?

We hope you'll appreciate that even just using the word grid, there's great potential for generating questions and exploring concepts. That potential is enhanced when children are encouraged to make picture and word grids of their own.

Activity: Infoscraps

This technique uses pieces of information written out on scraps of paper. Children work in groups, each group being supplied with a set of 'infoscraps' and one or more tasks. The value of using scraps of paper is that groups can physically manipulate the information to organise, reorganise, sequence, discard and so on, working with the scraps on a tabletop. The activity encourages the exploration of an issue through discussion and collaborative learning.

This first example, 'A Question of Energy' Figure 5.3, involves the thinking skills of listening, questioning, assessing, discriminating, reasoning, deciding and concluding.

Rhetorical Techniques

Here are the most common techniques to be found in so-called 'dodgy' arguments. Ask children to find any examples of one or more of them among the selection of infoscraps.

Persuader words – obviously, plainly, clearly, surely, undoubtedly (e.g. infoscraps 3, 25).

Emotive language – This is an attempt to influence people by the use of words which appeal to their feelings or which encourage particular associations (e.g. infoscraps 3, 36).

'Ad hominem' or 'argument against the man' – A personal attack on an individual, organisation or program which endorses a viewpoint (e.g. infoscrap 33).

Generalisation – A generalisation is a general notion or statement based on a few instances. It makes a universal claim and is often used disparagingly (e.g. infoscraps 3, 5, 25, 32, 34, 37).

'Ad populum' or 'appeal to the people.' The appeal is to the need to belong, to be accepted, be like everyone else and hold the views of the

A Question of Energy

1. Nuclear power stations can be built underground, but windfarms can't!

2. Wind turbines do not pollute the air, whereas fossil fuels do.

3. Cases of childhood asthma have been rising steadily over the years. Surely we all want clean energy for our children's health?

4. A huge amount of energy and materials are needed to build the number of wind turbines we'd require to supply sufficient energy. How can that be sensible?

5. Everyone would agree that nuclear fuels are more effective at generating energy than renewable alternatives.

6. Wind energy is free. Therefore our electricity bills will be tiny in comparison with what they are now!

7. Wind and wave energy are not called 'clean' technologies for nothing. Fossil fuels create greenhouse gases that contribute significantly to global warming.

8. Wind energy will never 'run out' but oil, gas and even nuclear fuel are in limited supply.

9. Nuclear energy is generated by using Uranium. There is estimated to be only 30–60 years' worth of Uranium left in the world, so it is not a 'renewable' fuel, as some people argue it to be.

10. My neighbour says whether or not to build more wind turbines is a no-brainer!

11. Wind turbines are big and ugly. Also, they are not silent but let out a low hum. I wouldn't want one built near my house.

12. We have got to solve the energy crisis or else future generations will struggle to survive.

13. Nuclear power stations generate only small amounts of greenhouse gases. Therefore, we should go nuclear.

14. The party I voted for supports clean energy; therefore, we should build wind farms.

15. My Auntie Edith loves her gas cooker. No way would she agree to build more wind farms.

16. Most of the gas we use is for industry, heating and lighting. Nuclear fuel can't replace that.

17. Most of the oil we use is for transport. How can nuclear power be used for that?

18. I once saw this film where nuclear radiation turned this man into a monster!

19. It is a known fact that none of the renewable energies – wind, solar, hydroelectric, etc. – can supply the world's increasing energy needs.

20. My uncle lives near a coal-burning power station and he's had a bad cough for years.

21. The cost of building wind turbines will fall as more and more are built.

22. Investing in renewable energy sources will make us more independent. We won't be at the mercy of oil-producing nations.

23. Underground nuclear power stations would be safer from attack by an enemy. Wind turbines could easily be destroyed.

24. Trees are a renewable resource, so why can't we build wood-burning power stations?

Figure 5.3, 5.4 and *5.5* These figures present a number of statements, in this case around the issue of nuclear energy versus fossil fuels versus renewables.

25. Clearly, the price of fossil fuels is steadily rising, which makes wind farms a more attractive option.

26. Greenhouse gases make global warming worse.

27. Not all scientists agree that global warming is caused by man.

28. The cost of building nuclear power stations will fall as more and more are built.

29. Wind turbines do not become less safe with age, whereas nuclear power stations do.

30. Fossil fuels are needed to mine nuclear fuel, so the nuclear power industry is not 'carbon free'

31. I read in a book that because of global warming, I'd be able to grow oranges in my back garden. That's great! (Oranges are so expensive!)

32. Most scientists agree that renewable energy technology is better for the planet than fossil fuels.

33. The Leader of Kenniston Council prefers the nuclear option, but there's a rumour he fiddles his expenses, so I'm not going to believe what he says!

34. Most sensible people in this country would vote for the safer option of renewable energy.

35. The Government is only interested in making the rich richer, so they'll go with whatever option achieves that.

36. Just imagine an orphaned child wandering around a city destroyed by a nuclear bomb – then tell me nuclear technology is safe!

37. Politicians have done nothing to sort out this country's long-term energy policy.

38. The simple fact is that we need to use renewable energy to cut greenhouse gases, otherwise our economy will eventually suffer.

39. Onshore wind power is proven to be reliable, efficient and cost-effective source. The latest government research shows that onshore wind is supported by a massive 66% of the public, with 12% opposed, including a meagre 4% who are strongly opposed.

40. Wind works that's a plain fact. To say wind energy is unreliable is simply wrong – a case of people believing what they want to believe without checking the figures.

41. Offshore wind turbines are expensive at the moment because they're new technology. But the more we build them, the cheaper and more reliable they'll become as a way of generating electricity.

42. In Germany, individuals and communities own most wind turbines, while in Britain, most are owned by big companies. So, in Germany, there is a greater sense of community ownership and, therefore, less opposition to wind power.

Figure 5.3, 5.4 and 5.5 (Continued)

majority – as in 'Most sensible people in this country would feel the same way' (e.g. infoscraps 5, 12, 34, 42).

Appeal to authority – Referring to authority figures, sometimes in a vague or generalised way, to back up an argument – 'Many scientists now feel that enough evidence has been gathered to conclude that . . .' (e.g. infoscraps 27, 32).

Appeal to cost – The cost of something is often quoted as a reason for not doing it or indeed to go ahead if the costs seem reasonable or can be recouped. It is one thing to cost something objectively and to decide after due consideration that it is too expensive. It is quite another to use the question of cost as a way of avoiding all analysis or argument (e.g. infoscraps 4, 21, 25, 28, 41).

Factual inaccuracy – Use of (possibly) inaccurate facts relies on the reader not having the time or not being bothered to check them (e.g. infoscraps 9, 39. Note that generalisations can be a kind of factual inaccuracy, as in infoscraps 3, 16, 17).

Use of statistics and studies – It is very important to look at their source and how they are used to determine whether they validate an argument (e.g. infoscraps 9, 39).

Reducing viewpoints to a general or ideological perspective – e.g. the members of this political party are Euro-skeptics, while this other party is Pro-Europe (e.g. infoscraps 35, 37).

Rhetorical questions – Asked for effect rather than to prompt further thought. Often used with 'persuader' words (e.g. infoscraps 3, 17).

Shaky reasoning – The suspect use of if-then, so, therefore, it follows, etc., to give the effect of a valid reasoned connection (e.g. infoscraps 6, 13).

Sorting for Relevance

Ask the children to sift out infoscraps that they consider to be irrelevant to the issue, together with the reasons for their choices. Then the same groups pick three or four infoscraps they consider as having high relevance – these might be arguing for renewable energy sources or nuclear. Again, ask for the reasons behind their choices.

Extension Activities.

Ask the children to use some of the aforementioned techniques to create infoscraps around a different debatable topic.

Activity: Letter to the Editor

Teresa Green feels very strongly about the issue of energy and global warming. Ask the class to pick out the 'dodgy argument' techniques she uses when putting her viewpoint across. Some of them are mentioned previously, but there are others – see the annotated version of the letter that follows.

Don't Blame Me!

Dear Sir – Following your article in last week's paper, 'We Can All Do Our Bit' – I bitterly resent the suggestion that I am not doing everything I can to protect our environment. For instance, I strongly object to being lumped together with people who treat the environment like a dustbin – the eco-vandals who drop litter, who fly-tip, who leave lights on around the home unnecessarily or, almost as bad, leave electrical equipment on standby rather than switching it off when not in use... The list is infinite! We are bombarded endlessly on TV and in the newspapers about being 'environmentally friendly' so surely, people must have gotten the message by now? Most of them have, of course, which means that their polluting habits and lifestyles must simply boil down to laziness and selfishness!

Your article goes on to take an extremely patronising tone over the issue of renewable energy versus the use of nuclear and fossil fuels – as though the debate was already settled and only sensible, intelligent and caring people would opt for renewables. It is not, of course, not by a long way. Not all scientists agree that renewable energy technologies like wind turbines and solar panels constitute the best way forward. Besides that, wind turbines are big, ugly structures that ruin our environment visually, while solar panels in the quantities needed cover huge areas of land that would be better given over to crops or for grazing. Nuclear power stations, on the other hand, can be built small and efficient – the more the world wants them, the better the designs will get. *And* they can be constructed underground, out of sight and out of harm's (i.e. terrorists') way.

Another point (which I don't suppose many people have thought about) is that *any* technology able to offer cheap and near-endless supplies of energy will only encourage the kind of mindless energy use that plagues us at the moment. When there are yet *more* cars (even electric ones), *more* gadgets, *more* lights, then huge quantities of waste heat will be produced and pumped out into the atmosphere. Talk about global warming!

In conclusion, then, I hope that your readers (being sensible and caring people) realise that I at least am doing my bit to help prevent the world from becoming a dried-up wilderness unfit for human habitation.

Yours faithfully, Teresa Green, Tooting Bec.

Annotated version:

Dear Sir – Following your article in last week's paper, 'We Can All Do Our Bit' – I bitterly (1) resent the suggestion that I am not doing everything I can to protect our environment. For instance, I strongly (2) object to being lumped (3) together with people who treat the environment like a dustbin – the eco-vandals (4) who drop litter, who fly-tip, who leave lights on around the home unnecessarily (5) or, almost as bad, leave electrical equipment on standby rather than switching it off when not in use... The list is infinite! (6) We are bombarded endlessly (7) on the TV and in the newspapers about being 'environmentally friendly' so surely people (8/9) must have gotten the message by now? (10) Most of them have of course, which means that their polluting habits and lifestyles must simply boil down to laziness and selfishness! (11)

Your article goes on to take an extremely (12) patronising tone over the issue of renewable energy versus the use of nuclear and fossil fuels – as though the debate was already settled and only sensible, intelligent and caring people would opt for renewables. It is not, of course, not by a long way (13). Not all scientists agree (14) that renewable energy technologies like wind turbines and solar panels constitute the best way forward. Besides that, wind turbines are big, ugly structures that ruin our environment visually, while solar panels in the quantities needed cover huge areas of land that would be better given over to crops or for grazing. Nuclear power stations, on the other hand, can be built small and efficient – the more the world wants them, the better the designs will get (15). *And* (16) they can be constructed underground, out of sight and out of harm's (i.e. terrorists') way.

Another point (which I don't suppose many people have thought about) is that *any* technology able to offer cheap and near-endless supplies of energy will only encourage the kind of mindless energy use that plagues us at the moment. When there are yet *more* cars (even electric ones), *more* gadgets, *more* lights, (17) then huge quantities of waste heat will be produced and pumped out into the atmosphere. Talk about global warming!!

In conclusion, then, I hope that your readers (being sensible and caring people) (18) realise that I at least am doing my bit to help prevent the world from becoming a dried-up wilderness unfit for human habitation.

1. emotive language
2. emotive language
3. metaphor used for its emotional impact
4. a 'catchy phrase' that uses overstated metaphor ('vandals') for effect
5. repetition for rhetorical effect
6. exaggeration
7. metaphor and exaggeration used for emotional impact
8. persuader word 'surely'
9. appeal to the people/generalisation
10. rhetorical question
11. unsupported assertion
12. exaggeration

13. unsupported assertion
14. appeal to authority
15. shaky reasoning
16. underlining for emphasis
17. italics for emphasis and repetition (the pattern of three) for rhetorical effect
18. appeal to the people

Debating Tactics

The tricks and techniques used earlier also appear frequently in debates/discussions. Children can listen critically to note when they are being used and counter them by asking searching questions...

'Everyone would agree that nuclear fuels are more effective at generating energy than renewable alternatives.' How do you know that everyone would agree? And where is the evidence that nuclear fuels are more effective than renewables?

'Wind energy is free. Therefore, our electricity bills will be tiny in comparison with what they are now!' How is wind energy free? What about the cost of building and maintaining wind turbines? Even if wind energy was free, how would you work out that our electricity bills would be 'tiny' as a result? Wouldn't energy companies and their investors want to keep prices and, therefore, profits as high as possible?

'There is estimated to be only 30–60 years' worth of Uranium left in the world, so it is not a 'renewable' fuel, as some people argue it to be.' Where did you get this figure?

'The party I voted for supports clean energy; therefore, we should build wind farms.' What does the party you voted for actually say about renewable energy versus nuclear and/or fossil fuels? Why does it follow that we should build windfarms? And who are 'we'?

'My uncle lives near a coal-burning power station and he's had a bad cough for years.' Are you suggesting a link between the power station and your uncle's cough? Are there other factors that might affect his cough? How common do you think it is that burning coal causes coughs to develop? And how could you find out?

'Clearly, the price of fossil fuels is steadily rising, which makes wind farms a more attractive option.' How is it clear? Where did you get that idea from? What are the costs of developing wind turbine technology that make it a 'more attractive option'?

'Not all scientists agree that global warming is caused by man.' Which ones do not? What are the reasons for their disagreement? Which areas of science do they specialise in and, therefore, are they qualified to speak with authority?

Children can also use the following 'ploys' to challenge an opponent in a debate and for strengthening their own case –

Answering a point with a question
Questioning the meaning of words
What-if counter example
Eliciting a personal opinion

To consolidate the aforementioned, arrange a class discussion around some appropriate topic and encourage the children to notice and point out these tactics. Tip: Children can actually mention the tactic they are using (a kind of 'annotated debate'), bearing in mind the epithet often used in philosophy sessions that they can be merciless in the pursuit of truth but merciful, i.e. respectful, with the one who is making the point.

Note: What we've said about debating tactics is fairly sophisticated and might well be more appropriate for older pupils. Advice for teaching debating skills to younger children can be found on YouTube.

Activity: A Raft of Problems

This example explores the so-called 'Lifeboat Dilemma'. One version of this describes the scenario of an ocean liner that is sinking. An available lifeboat has room for ten people, but 15 passengers still remain on the ship. This means that five will have to put on life jackets and jump into the sea. The water is very cold and no one can survive in it for more than 15 minutes.

Split the class into five groups. Explain to the children that for most of the tasks they are allowed to make a personal choice, but it would also be useful if they could also offer a group choice where a measure of agreement has been reached. Emphasise that, as far as possible, choices and decisions should be supported by reasons.

The Infoscraps.

1) people should be picked by drawing straws.
2) people should be picked by age.
3) people should be picked by how rich they are.
4) people should be picked by gender.
5) people should be picked by how powerful or influential they are.
6) people should be picked based on their achievements in life.
7) people should be picked by nationality.
8) people should be picked according to their religion.
9) people should be picked depending on their colour.

More Challenging Activities

10) people should be picked depending on how good or evil they are.
11) people should be picked according to how healthy they are.
12) people should be picked depending on how truthful they are.
13) people should be picked according to how many others depend on them.
14) people should be picked according to their weight.
15) the stowaway should be saved.
16) the illegal immigrant should be saved.
17) children should be saved before adults.
18) women should be saved before men.
19) people I like should be saved before people I dislike.
20) the kinds of people I don't like should not be saved.
21) people from a country we're at war with should not be saved.
22) the strongest should be saved.
23) one passenger has an incurable disease.
24) one passenger is a spy.
25) one passenger is your friend.
26) one passenger is a thief.
27) one passenger is pregnant.
28) one passenger might be pregnant.
29) one passenger is an Olympic rowing champion.
30) one passenger is yourself.
31) two passengers have recently become engaged.
32) one passenger, recently engaged, is marrying for money.
33) one passenger is a Member of Parliament.
34) one passenger is a young mother with her baby.
35) one passenger has just won a fortune in the lottery.
36) one passenger is a priest.
37) one passenger is a nun.
38) one passenger is a doctor.
39) one passenger is a midwife.
40) one passenger is a TV celebrity.

Tasks:
Encourage children to question the clarity of the infoscraps. For instance, scrap 3 says, 'People should be picked by how rich they are.' Firstly, ask children to consider what 'rich' means. How much wealth does someone need to have before they are labelled rich? Further, how could wealth in itself justify priority in allowing someone to board the lifeboat? Similarly, infoscrap 5 states, 'People should be picked by how powerful or influential they are' but does that mean physically powerful, politically powerful, etc.? Develop the thinking by using 'if-then': If someone was physically powerful, then what benefits might that bring if he or she were allowed on board the lifeboat?

Explore the idea of 'strength of reasons' (see page 9). Opinions and conclusions should always be backed by reasons. However, these can vary in robustness and therefore in their persuasive power. So, for example, if it's decided that 'People should be picked by how rich they are' the following reasons might be given in support –

1. Rich people have worked hard for their money, so they deserve to live to enjoy the rewards of their efforts.
2. Rich people who are saved might be so grateful that they give lots of money to charities such as Air Ambulance or the Royal National Lifeboat Institution.
3. Rich people who own businesses employ lots of workers. If such a rich person died, the businesses might be sold off and many employees could lose their jobs.
4. Rich people have no greater right to be saved than the less well-off.
5. Rich people can afford private medical care, more expensive medicines, etc. Therefore they are likely to live longer and so have more time to do good deeds if they are saved.
6. Rich people contribute more to society in the form of taxes, so if they were not saved, society would lose out.

Show children the list of reasons and ask them to rate the statements on a scale of 1–6, where one means a weak and unconvincing reason and six means a strong and highly convincing reason. Point out to the class that a 'reason' implies that some reasoning/considering has been done to reach a conclusion.

Ask the class to analyse the statements for flaws, weaknesses, unsupported opinions and non sequiturs (statements that do not follow logically from previous statements). So with regard to the reasons mentioned earlier –

1a. Some rich people have worked hard for their money. In other cases wealth may have been gained by inheritance, through gambling, crime, etc. So while rich people may in some cases deserve (a word to explore) to enjoy their wealth, riches by themselves should not give them priority for being saved.
2a. This is 'maybe thinking' – pure speculation not backed by reasoned argument.
3a. Perhaps the business of a rich person would be sold off if he or she died. In many cases, the workforce would be retained. For those employees who were not, there may be redundancy or relocation packages. For workers on zero-hour contracts or who otherwise have few rights, they might simply find themselves out of work. This situation is a matter for unions and politicians to act upon.

Also, if people become rich by exploiting workers in this way, it is no argument for allowing them to board the lifeboat in preference to others.

4a. Morally it is correct that rich people have as much right to be saved as those less well-off. In other words therefore, wealth should not be a factor in deciding who boards the lifeboat.

5a. The fact that rich people may live longer than those less wealthy is no guarantee that because of this they will bring more good into the world. We could argue that any rich person might leave a lot of money to good causes in the event of their death.

6a. Some rich people pay taxes fairly, while others perhaps try to avoid taxes. Also, when a wealthy person dies an inheritance tax is payable to the government, which (in an ideal world) would be put towards the betterment of society.

Invite the children to come up with any reasons of their own to support the chosen statement on the infoscrap.

Give each group infoscraps 1–22 and a copy of the Agreement Line, Figure 5.6 (or ask them to draw one for themselves on a large sheet of paper). Ask the groups to decide how far they agree that the passengers mentioned on the infoscraps should be saved. Encourage children to support their conclusions with reasons.

Give each group infoscraps 23–40 and a copy of the Likelihood Line, Figure 5.7. Ask the groups to decide whether they would save the people mentioned on the infoscraps.

Strongly Agree	
Mildly Agree	
Not Sure	
Mildly Disagree	
Strongly Disagree	

Figure 5.6 The image simplifies children's thinking as to how far they agree-disagree with particular viewpoints.

Definitely

Probably

Possibly

Not Sure

Possibly Not

Probably Not

Definitely Not

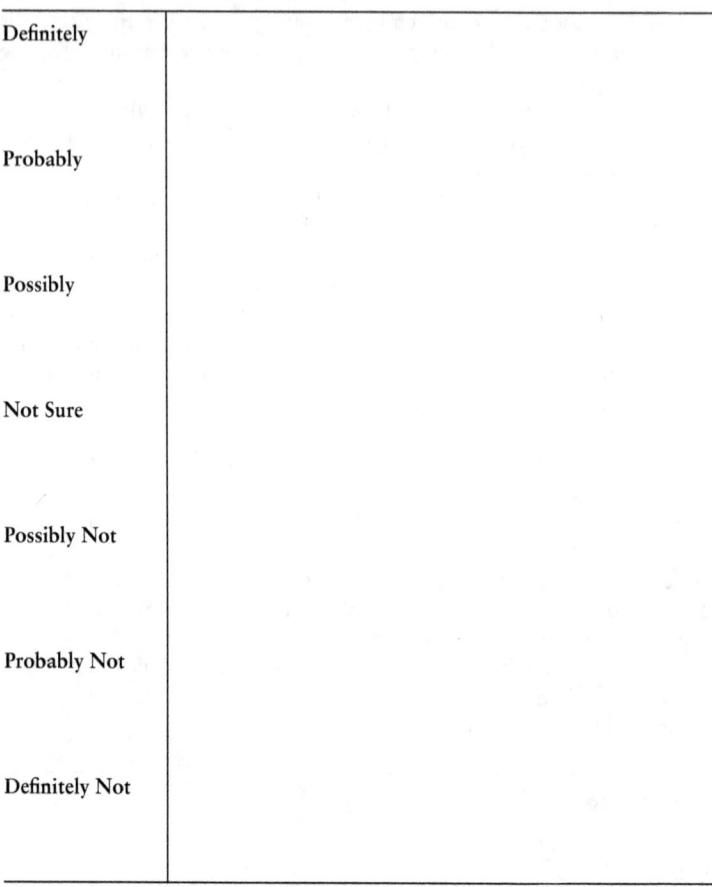

Figure 5.7 This activity is used in conjunction with Figure 5.6, the Agreement Line, where children are asked to decide how likely a particular scenario might be.

Again, use infoscraps 23–40. In this task, two infoscraps refer to the same person in the following combinations. Ask children how the extra information influences their decisions –

- 23 + 25 (so a passenger has an incurable disease and is your friend, etc.)
- 28 + 32
- 23 + 34
- 31 + 32
- 26 + 38

Ask children to combine infoscraps for themselves in this way. Children may want to do the task individually, but we think they would benefit from working with a partner or in a small group. Allow children to use infoscraps 15–40. Once a pair or group has created an infoscrap combination, instruct them to swap it with another group. Does the extra piece of information about the chosen passenger influence the group for or against saving that person or does it have no bearing on the issue?

Take It Further – If-Then

If-Then. Ask children to pick an infoscrap and apply 'if-then thinking' to it. Ask for as many if-thens as possible. So, for example –

Infoscrap 26 'One passenger is a thief.'
Starting position – I think people who are good deserve to be saved ahead of people who do bad things.
If he stole medicines to help his sick child, then I think he deserves more to be saved.
If he stole from a friend, then I think he deserves less to be saved.
If he stole to buy drugs to sell to children, then I think he is a lot less deserving to be saved.

You can extend the activity further by inviting children to challenge one or more of the statements, remembering that while someone may strongly disagree with another's opinion, they must be respectful of that person at all times.
So with regard to the less deserving/more deserving statements, they could be challenged in these ways –

Some religions teach that all life is sacred, so how could someone be condemned to death for having stolen something in the past? What if that person has worked hard to atone for his or her sins?
How many of us have never stolen something at some time in our lives? Do you think a person is less deserving of being saved because of the act of theft, the thing that was stolen, the reason for stealing or all, some or none of these?
You believe that 'If he stole from a friend then I think he less deserves to be saved.' What if the friend was going to cheat in an exam and what was stolen was the crib note? Then the thief would have stolen it because what the friend was doing was wrong and/or to save the friend from getting into trouble if he was caught.

You say that 'If he stole to buy drugs to sell to children then I think he is a lot less deserving to be saved.' But here you have made the assumption that the drugs were things like ecstasy or heroin etc. What if the drugs were medicines that would make sick children well again?

Some further points to ponder.

Ask the children to think about and discuss the following. Use the agreement line to assess the strength of the children's feelings.

The people who have brought the greatest good to the world in their lives should be saved first.

Because all human lives are precious it is impossible to decide who should be saved.

'The greatest good or happiness for the greatest number' is a rule that should be applied in deciding who should be saved. The rule considers what good or bad consequences might result from any chosen action.

The captain of the ship should decide who boards the lifeboats.

Women and children should board the lifeboats first.

The captain should go down with his or her ship.

Notes:

A child in one Y6 group who tackled this dilemma suggested that everyone strong and healthy enough should take turns going into the water and then spend some time in the lifeboat to recover. That way, those concerned take a fair share of risk and responsibility in helping the whole group to survive.

'Ethics' comes from the Greek meaning 'the science of morals'; from 'ethos' meaning the spirit or characteristics of a community, culture or era that reflects its attitudes and aspirations.

'Dilemma' comes from the Greek words 'di' (twice) and 'lemma' (premise or assumption). The phrase 'on the horns of a dilemma' means trying to choose between two unfavourable outcomes.

The so-called 'lifeboat dilemma' was used by the American ecologist and philosopher Garrett Hardin as an analogy to explore issues of overpopulation on what was then fashionably called Spaceship Earth. Hardin's arguments amounted to a case for *not* helping the populations of poorer countries, so a highly racist standpoint. For more details, go to www.garretthardinsociety.org/articles/art_lifeboat_ethics_case_against_helping_poor.html.

Hardin's reasoning is robust and challenging and, for us, it constantly created an uneasy tension between what might be seen as the 'logically' right thing to do and what the heart causes us to agonise over.

Ethical dilemmas are a powerful way of exploring ideas such as right and wrong, justice and conscience as well as developing reasoning and debating skills. Martin Cohen's '101 Ethical Dilemmas' presents some classic dilemmas with accompanying commentary. See Bibliography.

Activity: The Trolley Problem

This is a famous ethical dilemma. Ask children to imagine that a railway trolley is plunging downhill out of control. At the bottom of the hill the railway line branches in two directions. On one branch six people have been tied to the rails by a villain who has chosen this melodramatic way to rid himself of his enemies. On the other branch a person illegally crossing the line has tripped and been knocked out, lying sprawled across the tracks. It so happens that you have been walking nearby and are passing the manual points that can send the runaway trolley along one branch or the other. What do you do? Doing nothing also counts as a decision.

Various commentators have suggested that the trolley problem has no satisfactory solution but rather is designed to explore one's moral sense and test one's reasoning ability.

As well as discussing the dilemma with the class, ask children to create infoscraps around the scenario to extend their exploration. Two thinking tools – 'what if' and 'if-then' – should make it easier for children to have ideas. So, for example –

What if the unconscious person started to come around and might realise the danger in time?

If one of the six people tied up was a distant cousin, would that affect your decision?

What if you knew that the unconscious person had once stolen money from you?

If you knew you had a 50% chance of surviving if you leapt aboard the speeding trolley to apply the brakes, would you attempt it?

Activity: Quizzing the Text

It's reasonable to assume that authors choose their words deliberately to create a certain impression and reaction in the reader; so-called 'author intention' or 'authorial intent'. Point this out to the children, then show them a piece of text and invite them to ask questions to deepen their understanding of the writing. Many of the questions are likely to focus on what children don't know; what certain words or sentences mean. Possible answers can be discussed or researched. Emphasise again that not knowing an answer, but wanting to find out, is an educationally 'healthy' behaviour.

As an example, we've chosen Thomas Hardy's poem 'The Darkling Thrush' which is readily accessed online. Questions children might come up with could include –

What does 'darkling' mean? Is it the same as 'darkening' and if so, why didn't the poet say 'darkening'?

What is a coppice gate?

Why does the poet start 'Frost' and 'Winter's' with a capital letter?

What are bine-stems?

What does 'fervourless' mean?

How is the poem meant to make the reader feel? Is that how I feel?

Another activity, when children have a grasp of what the poem means, is to ask them to write the gist of it in ordinary, non-poetic language – an outrage perhaps to poetry lovers, but the task helps to clarify the children's understanding and the ease with which they can explain the meaning to others.

Activity: The Moon Cannot Be Stolen

A linked activity is to take the gist of a story, for example, the tale of Ryokan and the thief on page 62 and below and to expand it into a more detailed story after asking any questions to deepen children's understanding. So, for example –

What is a traditional story?

What is a parable?

What is a Zen master?

In what sense could Ryokan have possibly 'given' the moon to the thief?

In a slightly more extended version of the story, Ryokan has taken some fruit and vegetables that he's grown to the market to trade for sandals to replace his old and worn-out pair. Ryokan's produce is nowhere near worth enough to procure the sandals, but the sandal maker takes pity on Ryokan and gives him the sandals anyway, hoping that one day Ryokan

More Challenging Activities 111

will find a way to lift himself out of poverty. At this, Ryokan smiles and tells the sandal maker that actually he has all the riches he needs. The thief as he passes by overhears this, follows Ryokan home and while Ryokan tends to his garden, sneaks into the house to look for these 'riches'. The rest of the story is as previously told.

These added details give us more insight into Ryokan's beliefs and values and why he finds the moon so beautiful.

Help children to add detail to the longer version by prompting them with further questions and suggestions –

What might Ryokan, the sandal maker and the thief have looked like?

Describe the bustling market, not just visually; include sounds and smells. Remember that the story is set long ago in China so you may need to do some research.

What fruit and vegetables could Ryokan have taken to trade?

Briefly describe Ryokan's journey home.

What did Ryokan's hut look like, inside and out?

How might the thief have felt when he realised there was nothing valuable to steal?

Briefly describe the moonlit landscape, which would add to Ryokan's appreciation.

Activity: Interrogate the Speaker

Here, children are presented with an account or anecdote and are then invited to ask questions about it. The account might be a written one and the speaker might not be present, though that doesn't stop children from framing the questions. A variation is to have the class teacher or another adult volunteer or volunteers acting together, to role-play someone with a certain and perhaps controversial viewpoint, who can then reply to questions to try and justify or at least explain that viewpoint.

This first example is a strange experience Steve had some years ago. At the time, his wife was running a children's day nursery based in a large house they had converted that dated back to around 1912. His wife chose the place not just because it suited their purposes but because, as she said, 'it felt right'. On one occasion, a friend came round one evening: he and Steve were sitting in the lounge, which doubled as a staff room (empty of staff just then) and as Steve was talking to him realised that the friend wasn't paying attention. Instead, he was staring towards the corner of the room to the right of the fireplace. Steve tapped his arm and he startled, then apologised –

'I'm sorry I wasn't listening. I was distracted watching your ghost.'

When Steve questioned him about this, he said quite adamantly but also matter-of-factly that the ghost of an old lady was present on the first floor. 'She's very benign. She comes in through the main door here, walks diagonally across the room and disappears through the wall to the right of the fireplace.'

Steve had no reason to doubt that his friend was sincere and that he thought he'd just experienced something unusual. Steve could easily have dismissed what he'd said, except for two things – why would he bother to make it up? His sense of humour didn't work that way. And also, while Steve and his wife were living in the house before the nursery conversion was completed, they had an old cat that used to cuddle up to one of them when they sat in that room of an evening watching TV. On a number of occasions Stubby (yes, really) would suddenly become alert, sit up and look slowly at the main door, then track something they couldn't see diagonally across the room towards the right-hand corner. After this, she'd settle back down again.

A sceptic is likely to dismiss the whole thing as a coincidence and suggest perhaps that the friend was pulling Steve's leg. But what happened, coupled with Steve's wife's sensitivity to the atmosphere of a place, gives pause for thought.

Now, invite the class to come up with questions to ask if Steve was in their classroom. Since the replies might prompt further questions, here are responses to some of the questions he's been asked in the past about the 'The old lady ghost' experience . . .

What do you think happened?
I see no reason to doubt that my friend experienced something. Sceptics might say he was hallucinating, having a particularly vivid daydream perhaps or that he was indeed joking. But his matter-of-fact manner and the way the cat behaved on a number of occasions stretch the idea of coincidence rather too far for me. Also, I question again why he would bother to tell me a made-up story.

So, do you believe in ghosts?
I think that there are a number of explanations for what we call ghosts, including fraud, lies, misperceptions as well as possibly supernatural causes. I'll add that the terms 'supernatural' and 'paranormal' (beyond the normal) are used based on what some people regard to be natural and normal. Many scientists feel that matter and energy

make up all of reality – i.e. that the physical universe and the 'laws' that govern it are what counts as normal. Any explanation of ghosts and other such phenomena, therefore, need to be explained in purely physical terms.

So, you think that the supernatural exists?

I will go so far as to say that human beings still have a lot to learn about the universe. For instance, what we see in the sky is only around 4–5% of what exists. The other 95% or 96% is made up of so-called dark matter and dark energy – 'dark' because they can't be seen and about which scientists know very little. My friend Douglas Hill (also see page 72) once co-authored a successful book about the supernatural but then switched to writing children's fiction. When I asked him why he stopped writing books on supernatural topics, he said tantalisingly, 'because I found out too much.'

Had your friend tried to pull your leg at other times?

No, not before or since. If he was the joker or trickster type, that would have made me doubt what he told me. But he said it all so casually.

And you say that your wife is sensitive to atmospheres?

Whenever we've been house hunting, the way a place 'feels' has always been important to her. It works both ways: something odd happened many years ago. I had been invited to run a writing workshop for schoolchildren over a weekend. The venue was Ford Castle, a very old and very grand building in Northumberland. My wife came with me to relax and enjoy the area. We arrived several hours before the pupils and the warden showed us around. At one point, he stopped in front of an oak door and said, 'I know that some children prefer to write sprawled out on the floor rather than sitting at a table. And so . . .'

With a grand gesture he pushed open the door to reveal a large, bare room with dark wooden panelling, tall arched windows and a plush red fitted carpet. He stepped inside and I followed. My wife put one foot over the threshold before drawing quickly back. She looked scared. She said, 'I can't go in there. It feels bad. Something horrible happened in that room.' The warden asked if she had read the castle's guidebook, but of course she hadn't. We knew nothing about the castle beforehand. Looking slightly astonished, the warden told us that centuries ago two people had been murdered in that very room. I'll also mention that there's a 10th-century church in a village some miles from where we live that my wife won't go anywhere near because it gives her 'bad vibes'. (www.ford-and-etal.co.uk/history-heritage/ford-castle/)

Could the way your wife felt about the room have just been a coincidence?

Why should she have reacted in that way to just that one room? We were shown around the rest of the building and she had no reaction at all to any of the other rooms. Anyway, coincidence as an explanation isn't really much of an explanation at all – it falls into the 'nothing but' category where it's used to explain away an experience, especially by people who don't accept the idea of the paranormal. How likely is it that my wife should have had that dark impression at the exact moment she stepped over the threshold of that room where the murders took place? In other words, is the idea of coincidence at all credible?

So, do you think that the spirits of the murdered people still haunt that room?

I don't know. As I've said, I think there are a number of explanations behind what we call ghosts. Some people think that the 'energy' of violent events can somehow be absorbed by the environment, the so-called 'stone tape theory', although there's no scientific evidence for that (yet). And it would be difficult to find evidence of what some people experience. I've no doubt if my wife could be persuaded to go into that room again, she'd have the same dark feeling, but scientifically that just counts as anecdotal evidence rather than the repeatability of an event that's necessary for science to prove or disprove that something is so. I wonder then if it's reasonable to conclude that, truly speaking, the experience lies outside the province of science, so science should really have nothing to say about it. In other words, to say my wife's experience was a hallucination or coincidence or whatever would be someone's opinion and not a scientific statement. So while science can demonstrate that hallucinations exist, it can't prove that what my wife felt was a hallucination.

Do you believe your wife?

I believe that she really had those dark feelings and I discount coincidence as an explanation. How likely is it that she'd have the impression that people were murdered in that room just at that moment when she set foot in the room where people had indeed been killed and without any previous knowledge at all of Ford Castle? Saying that, a sceptic might put my wife's reaction down to 'cryptomnesia' or hidden memories. The reasoning behind this is that at some point in her life, my wife read about Ford Castle and that room then forgot the information, which lay hidden subconsciously until the recall was triggered by actually being at Ford Castle. But if that was so, why didn't the information just pop into mind as recalled facts; that is, without the dark feelings that were strong enough to prevent her from going into the room? If hidden memory was the explanation, wouldn't it be more likely that she'd go into the room and say something like, 'Oh,

I've just remembered. Some people were murdered in this room a few hundred years ago.' However, that recollection is very specific: she would need to have remembered that it was in this particular room that the murders occurred. Also, no other facts popped into mind as we toured the rest of the building. So what an incredible coincidence that her only hidden memory on that day happened just as we came to the red-carpeted room. I'm sceptical about the sceptic's hidden memory explanation!

However, take a sceptical point of view. Can you suggest any other explanations of the experience, backed by strong reasons as far as possible? So, if one explanation is that the lady is lying, why would she do that: why would she pretend to be fearful of stepping into the room? Also, remember that Steve and the castle guide were present too. To lie convincingly, she would have needed to find out about the murder in the room. But what if the incident never happened and Steve made it up so he could write about it in this book? Why might he have done this?

If you choose to run the activity using role play, pick a topic that's a little controversial and not too emotive if you're working with primary-age children. If you select something like the earlier story, you might take a hardened sceptical point of view or that of someone who's open-minded or that of a 'believer'. We'll add that the dialogue is richer if another adult takes part and adopts a different viewpoint from yours.

Note: Some parents object to their children hearing anything about the paranormal and even disapprove of Fantasy fiction. So you might regard the example – based on an actual experience – as simply illustrating the way the activity works.

'Interrogate the Speaker' is also a great opportunity to use the tactics or 'moves' that are to be found in debates and philosophical enquiries. To illustrate this, here's an extract from a conversation between children and a teacher who is role-playing the opinion that all cars should be banned.

Pupil: Why do you think that?
Teacher: Because cars add massively to carbon emissions that cause climate change.
P: Some people don't believe in climate change.
T: I don't care about those other people's beliefs. Many ordinary people think climate change is real and many experts tell us that climate change is real and that global warming is getting worse. (Appeal to the populace and appeal to authority)
P: But do you think there's enough evidence to prove that climate change is happening?
T: Surely it's obvious because of the many and increasing number of extreme weather events we see so often in the news? (Rhetorical question)

P: The world's climate has been changing for millions of years, sometimes getting hotter and sometimes cooler. What's to say that the current warming is just natural, just a phase?

T: I think it's better to believe that human beings are causing climate change so that we can try and do something about it. Getting rid of cars right across the world would prevent millions of tonnes of polluting gases from going into the atmosphere. (Reasoning) Also, if global warming is a natural process and not man-made, the other arguments and reasons for getting rid of cars still stand.

P: Some people have to use cars for their work for instance.

T: Yes, there would have to be exceptions and of course ambulances, fire engines, police cars and other essential vehicles would remain. (Making distinctions) But with the world's population increasing more and more people will want to use cars, so the situation can only get worse. (Assumption – or sound reasoning? Also, perhaps, catastrophising)

P: What about other kinds of transport – aeroplanes, for instance? (Widening the discussion with a further example)

T: If I had my way, then all air travel for leisure would end, with exceptions perhaps being buses, trains and ships. Aircraft too are massively polluting and increase the risk of all life being wiped out! (Use of extreme scenario for emotional effect) The fact is that we can't go on as we have been doing, transport-wise. Think about how many lives would be saved if road traffic was hugely reduced, cutting the number of tragic accidents way down. (Appeal to emotions) Also, notice how many cars go by with just the driver inside – all that tonnage of metal for transporting just one person in each case. What a waste . . .

'Interrogate the Speaker' can also be used to familiarise children with facts and ideas within a topic area you're studying. So biology and medicine would be the focus if you argued from the viewpoint of somebody opposed to vaccination while taking the role of a 'flat Earther'* creates the opportunity to explore ideas in physics and astronomy. (We've never used the anti-vax topic in this activity. If we did, we'd be interested to see parental reactions. Would anti-vax parents lodge a complaint against us or approve of an activity that sharpened their child's critical thinking/questioning abilities while allowing them to learn more about the subject?)

*A friend of ours recently said that the only thing that flat Earthers have to fear is sphere itself.

A variation of the activity is to tell a story that's mainly true – so-called 90% stories – the aim being to encourage children to ask questions and research as necessary to try and uncover the falsehoods and deceptions. A further way of extending the activity is to choose a suitable urban folk-tale – also called a friend of a friend (FOAF) tale because one tactic for making them sound more believable is to claim that you heard it from a friend, who, in turn heard it from a friend. An exploration of urban folk-tales, with child-appropriate examples, is to be found in 'Understanding the World Through Narrative.' If you're interested in urban folktales, we recommend the collections by folklorist Jan Harold Brunvand.

Activity: New Earth

Ask children to imagine that they are part of a large group of colonists that are about to travel to an Earth-like world orbiting a nearby star. A huge amount is known about this world, named Terra Nova, although the colonists have not yet been fully briefed. It will also be up to them to organise themselves in various ways when they get there.

Invite the children to ask questions about the planet itself and how they might mould themselves into the beginnings of society: if working with older children, you can introduce different political/social systems used to shape societies across the world. Either decide on the answers to questions yourself (somewhat like a games master in a fighting fantasy adventure) or use a two-colour counter to get yes-or-no answers to closed questions; or, of course, you can use both techniques. If a child asks an irrational question such as 'Will we need a leader?' then either don't gamble on a counter flip in case you get 'no' – unless the class can be very creative in suggesting alternatives; or put the question back to the class, 'What would be the consequences if you didn't have a leader or a council of leaders?'

You can also prompt discussion by asking how colonists might deal with criminals and what rules and laws would help the colony to run well. A good 'meaty' question to ask is, 'If no colonists had yet been selected, who would deserve to go and why?' – discussing the 'Lifeboat Dilemma' first will be useful preparation (page 102); or 'Who would be most essential in ensuring the success of the colony?'

Incidentally, a 1951 science fiction film called 'When Worlds Collide' touches on this very point. The movie is based on a novel of the same name, first published in 1933 by Philip Wylie and Edwin Balmer.

Other details can be added to the scenario –

Would you let an AI supercomputer govern the colony and make all the important decisions?

What if, after the colonists had landed, they discovered that an intelligent and peaceful species already lived there?

What if there was a breakaway group in the colony who wanted things to be run along different lines?

And of course you can encourage the children to come up with more scenarios of their own.

Although the 'New Earth' is a kind of hypothetical thought experiment, discussions are relevant to the real world. Exploring the concepts of politics, laws, evolving technology, nonhuman intelligence and so on helps children to hone their views in the 'safely distant' context of the fictional new world scenario. The activity also creates the opportunity to discuss the perennial issue of whether humanity should spend vast amounts of money to send people into space or focus more on solving the many problems that exist here on Earth.

(Note: The word 'or' is known as a false choice or a false dilemma since it creates the impression that only two options exist. With regard to the previous scenario – spend on manned space travel or problems on Earth – can children think of other options that begin to unpick the complexity of the issue? – Exploring shades of grey, though perhaps not as many as 50).

Different scenarios can take discussion in new directions. We've found that popular examples include –

What if hostile aliens invaded the Earth?

What if powerful world leaders decided who your friends must be?

What if there was a device that stopped you having bad thoughts?

What if you, and only you, could see up to a minute into the future? (You can increase the 'look ahead' time to generate more ideas.)

What if a totally immersive virtual world was created that was so much better than this one? For an annual subscription, you can be hooked up to the technology that will take you there, permanently if you wish, while servant robots would attend to your every need in the real world. Would you go there? Permanently, or just to visit? Older pupils may know of the Matrix movies, in which case the scenario will be familiar to them. Another horrifying story along similar lines is E.M. Forster's short story 'The Machine Stops' published in 1928. Rather than give you any spoilers, we urge you to read it for yourself (a copy to view is to be found at https://archive.org/details/e.-m.-forster-the-machine-stops_202008/mode/2up). If you're really interested, you might want to research the so-called 'brain in a vat' theory. Incidentally, Roald Dahl wrote a darkly humorous short story on this topic called 'William and Mary', found in his 'Tales of the Unexpected' collection. The topic is also explored in the first of Stephen Laws' 'Philosophy Files' books – How do I know the world isn't virtual?

Activity: Questions About Questions

Consolidate what children have learned about questioning by presenting them with a list of examples followed by a list of tasks to think about, framed in the form of further questions. It's not necessary for children to know the answers to any questions in the first list, but encourage discussion so they can form answers to the second list. So, for example –

1. What is the name of the street where you live?
2. Are children who have strict discipline at home more creative than children of parents who are easier-going?
3. Who discovered Pluto?
4. How do you know that a person is beautiful?
5. What will the weather be tomorrow?
6. How do you do?
7. What part of speech is the word 'like'?
8. Will you achieve the career you really want?
9. 10x10 =?
10. Who are you?

An immediate way of deciding whether, or by how much, children have sharpened up their thinking skills will emerge in any questions they ask about the list before you've even shown them the list below. Responses we've encountered include –

Say more about what you mean by 'strict' in question 2. Give some examples.

Do you mean physical beauty in question 4, a beautiful personality, both – or something else?

What does the second 'do' mean in question 6?

In question 10, what kind of information are you looking for?

You can either attempt to answer questions like these or pop them back by asking, 'What do *you* think?' Alternatively, suggest that the second list of questions might clear up these issues.

Which questions can you answer with complete certainty? Why can't you be certain about the other questions?

Which questions can be answered with facts? What other ways can you think of to answer the other questions?

How do you define a fact? How do you know it's a fact? (And are those two questions different or do they mean the same thing?)

Can facts change? Give examples of facts that can or have changed and ones that, as far as you can find out, will remain the same.

Are there any questions you could ask about the statement, 'It's a fact that I have a certain opinion about what makes a person beautiful?'

Do any of the questions need to be answered by experts? What is an expert? How would an expert know (you're not allowed to say 'because she's an expert' – that's circular reasoning: see page 124).

Further to this, invite children to come up with more questions to add to this second list.

6   Conducting a Discussion

Firstly we want to say that a discussion is not the same as a debate. Debates are usually competitive and the aim is to 'win' while a discussion is more of a cooperative exploration of a topic. It is also less formal than a philosophical enquiry, although in both cases, while conversation might be free-flowing, participants try to stick to the point or topic.

By way of preparation, discuss with the class the difference between a fact, an opinion and a belief. The etymology of these words is interesting: 'fact' is linked to factory and manufacture and derives from the Latin 'to make' and ultimately from Proto-European 'to put, place, set.' The implication is that facts are human constructs based on our observations of the world. These are deep philosophical waters swirling around an idea expressed by writer Anais Nin that we don't see things as they are but as *we* are. We have even come across the suggestion that Mathematics itself isn't 'built in' to the universe but is a human invention that allows us to better understand how the universe works.

The word opinion comes again from Latin, meaning to think or believe. We might consider whether anyone with an opinion must always believe it's right and true. This prompts us to consider the notions of scepticism, open-mindedness and dogma. Scepticism is the tendency to doubt, although such an attitude exists along a continuum. At one extreme we have dogmatic or hard scepticism (sometimes referred to as 'skepticism'), where someone will not change a view or belief despite any amount of evidence and even proof to the contrary. The origin of dogma is 'opinion' which offers a useful insight to its nature. An open-mindedly sceptical person, however, is prepared to look at the evidence and consider alternative ideas that may prompt a change of mind, though most healthily based on critical thinking and reasoning. One could argue that the other extreme is gullibility, where one is easily persuaded not just by supposed facts but by appeal to emotions, authority, antiquity and popularity–

'Anyone who cared would accept that's true.'
'Experts tell us this is true, so how can we argue with that?'

DOI: 10.4324/9781003608714-6

'This idea has been around for hundreds of years, so it must be true.'

'Most people believe this, so surely we can't doubt it?'

Beliefs in one sense are acts of faith that may be based on facts, opinions, personal experiences or a complex mingling of them all. Beliefs can also be strongly and firmly held or 'malleable'; liable to be changed in light of further experience and evidence. So for instance we believe that Tasmania exists even though we've never been there because the weight of evidence we've experienced about it is compelling. So we might consider if 'belief' in Tasmania is the same as, say, belief in God? A person who has had a transcendental or revelatory experience of a universal creative intelligence will almost certainly base a faith in God on that. Such an experience does of course become anecdotal ('a personal account') as soon as it's conveyed to someone else which, it might be argued, weakens its potency.

When teaching children how to conduct a discussion, it's important to emphasise that –

Respect must be shown to the other participants.

Opinions must be backed up by reasons.

Strong emotions must be kept in check. The best discussions amount to an exchange of views and must never degenerate into a shouting match.

As an extension of these points, keep an eye out for these tactics, which children might use deliberately or unwittingly –

Attacking the person. Because some opinions and beliefs are held passionately, it's easy to criticise someone who holds a contrary view. In the spirit of how a discussion ought to run, it's fine to challenge the view itself – based on reasoned argument – but personal comments should be set aside.

Generalising. Although someone using generalisations may think it strengthens their point, the tactic can easily be countered. For instance, if someone said that 'children spend too much time playing video games these days', this can be challenged by asking which children or do you mean all children, how much time is too much do you include all video games and what evidence have you got to back that opinion up? Many proverbs are generalisations – also see page 59. Show some to the class and ask the children to question them –

1. All is fair in love and war.
2. A wise man changes his mind sometimes, a fool never.
3. Beggars can't be choosers.
4. Delays are dangerous.

5. Enough is better than too much.
6. Great talkers are great liars.

While we're not saying that these morsels of wisdom are plain wrong, they do invite questions, including asking for or discussing the definitions of certain words such as fair and wise. Defining is one of the skills used in a philosophical enquiry, insofar as it demands clear language so that all the participants are using the same meaning of a concept. One way of practising this is to split the class into groups, give the groups the same word to define, allow them some talking time and then compare their definitions. A variation is to ask every child to write a suitable word on a scrap of paper, put them in an envelope – the scraps of paper, not the children – and draw them out one by one so that the class can discuss each one until there's consensus as to a reasonable definition. The activity can also be scaffolded: it's relatively easy to come up with a definition of 'cat' but more difficult to define 'Science'. More challenging concepts would, of course, require more time for discussion.

The False Choice

Also, see page 118. In his book 'How to Argue' Jonathan Herring quotes George W. Bush, who said when talking about the war or terror, 'You are either for us or against us.' This leaves just the two options of agreeing or disagreeing, whereas you might want to agree to some extent or be neither for nor against the proposal. Encourage children therefore to be aware of either-or and, when an example appears, to think about what middle ground might be possible.

Red Herrings

According to the website study.com, this term was first used in an article written by a journalist in 1807. He described a (probably fictional) story in which he used an actual red herring fish* to distract a dog from chasing a hare. The term then came to take on the more general meaning of a distraction in discussions often assuming the form of changing the subject or straying from the point or even suggesting doing something other than having the discussion. Sometimes, red herrings are used positively to avoid a controversial subject so that tempers don't become frayed, but within the context of a discussion that is going to continue, they can indicate a weakness that the person changing the subject is unable to defend his point robustly.

* Wikipedia tells us that there's no such thing as an actual red herring fish but that the term refers to a particularly strong kipper. Smoking a herring can turn the fish a reddish colour. The things you find out!

Circular Arguments

Also called circular reasoning, this tactic tries to prove itself by using its own conclusion as evidence. So for example, to say, 'He is the best person for that job because he was promoted to that job,' takes us round in a circle. Note also the tricky use of the 'because', which requires a reason to be appended to it, but in this case the reason has no credibility. Reasons, of course, can be strong and convincing or lame. If a child says, 'I haven't brought in my homework because it fell in the bath full of water,' it might be true, but it is more likely to be doubted. For the child to claim that he hasn't done his homework because his Mum was taken ill and had to go to hospital, where he stayed with her all evening again may or may not be true, but it is more likely to be believed (we think anyway), especially if the listener empathises with the child's alleged situation.

Use of Extreme Conclusions

This tactic uses extreme examples to try and support a point of view. Someone suggesting more funding for the NHS might argue that 'without greater funding, tens of thousands more people will die needlessly.' Again, this might be true, but a critically aware thinker would ask where that information came from. This links with the use of vagueness. The person making the previous comment might counter with, 'Well, many studies have shown . . .' or 'It's just a matter of common sense . . .' These again can be challenged by asking what studies, or how is it a matter of common sense? And what do you mean by 'common sense' anyway?

Extreme conclusions often point towards dire consequences. For example, 'If that new rail link doesn't go ahead, then roads will quickly become clogged such that journeys by car will soon be impossible.'

Other tactics exist, but we feel that these are the most common and the ones that can be most easily spotted.

Activity: Dissect the Question

Encourage children to probe questions more deeply when they seem vague or general. For instance, recently we came across a survey question which asked 'Do you believe in UFOs?' It's easy enough to

Conducting a Discussion 125

say yes, no or not sure (the only options offered in the survey), but the question can be picked apart so that more accurate or detailed responses can be given.

For a start, UFO refers to Unidentified Flying Objects. 'Flying' suggests purposeful direction, while 'Object' implies something physical. Also, the survey didn't suggest that UFOs could be natural phenomena, flying saucers or something else. Increasingly, people interested in the topic are calling these things UAPs, Unexplained Aerial Phenomena. This is a vaguer but less leading way of labelling whatever the phenomenon might be.

When we put the initial question to a school philosophy club, children came up with responses such as –

Unidentified by whom?

If I say yes, do you automatically assume I believe that aliens exist?

If you ask whether I believe aliens exist, do you mean intelligent beings?

If you ask whether I believe intelligent aliens have visited Earth, how could I know? Can you point to any evidence that suggests they have? And if so, is there any contrary evidence? (The debate around the Roswell crash of a supposed UFO in 1947 is a good example.)

Another benefit of such questions is to use them as stepping stones towards more abstract questions ripe for a philosophical enquiry; in this case taking the notion of intelligence to explore what exactly we mean by that. In the same philosophy club, one child wondered whether the Loch Ness Monster existed. This led to an interesting discourse on what it means for something to exist, including the tantalising idea that if something exists in the imagination only, can we still say that it exists? In other words, what happened here was that children probed deeper, beyond the notion of whether the Loch Ness Monster exists – from 'monster' to the more philosophically searching concept of existence.

Activity: Point of View

As with arguments, discussions usually involve people taking a particular point of view. Here is a list of statements around the topic of a proposed new housing development on the outskirts of a village. Ask children to look at these and –

Separate facts from opinions.
Identify statements that argue for the development, those that are opposed and any that are 'neutral'.

Pair up comments that directly contradict one another.
Discard statements that seem to be irrelevant, ideally supported by some reasoning as to why they are.
Attempt to pinpoint which statements from all sides of the discussion are most persuasive and why.

Pinpoint any rhetorical tactics that attempt to persuade. These include –

Direct address. Addressing comments to particular people or groups. Spot these by looking for pronouns such as you and your.
Verbs such as should, could, may, might, must, ought to and shall are designed to create a mood or impression. These are called modal verbs – modal in the sense of 'modulating', or bringing extra meaning to a verb. So 'Let's go to the park' acquires an extra detail if we say 'We must go to the park.'
Emotive language, which includes anecdotes aiming to deliver an emotional impact.
Reasoning, which includes the use of facts and statistics. These of course can be checked.
Appeal to authority, which might take the form of 'experts tell us that . . .' or 'many studies show . . .'
Imagery. Creating an image in participants' minds can have a powerful emotional impact. This tactic can also incorporate the use of simile, metaphor and exaggeration.
Repetition. Repeating a point can reinforce it. This move is related to the so-called 'power of three'. The well-known aphorism of 'say something three times and it's true' makes use of what's called the illusory truth effect. When children are aware of this they will more readily realise that repetition in itself doesn't necessarily make a statement any truer.
Flattery. Complimenting other participants also has an emotional effect and may make them more amenable to your viewpoint.
Imperative command. These are statements aimed at creating a sense of urgency, often coupled with the point (sometimes implied) that if things aren't done immediately then dire consequences will result.

Activity: New Housing Development

1. Villages ought to be peaceful places. Many people retire to a village to get away from the bustle of towns and cities.
2. My uncle lives in a village and he loves it.

Conducting a Discussion   127

3. I read an article recently which said that such large housing developments cause crime in the area to increase.
4. It's all very well building new houses, but what about the infrastructure like shops, schools and medical centres?
5. 'Infrastructure' only adds to the size of the development.
6. Even a small housing development is a creeping evil. If planning is granted for ten houses, what's to stop the developer from putting in further planning applications for even more houses?
7. We don't know what form this development will take – huge mansions for the wealthy or affordable housing for those people who want to get on the property ladder.
8. New housing destroys the sense of community. In the town where I live, you used to be able to walk down the High Street and recognise lots of people. Many of them would smile and say hello. But the town has grown so much that now there's just a sea of anonymous, unsmiling strangers.
9. People in the village where I live are really cliquey. And if you don't have a dog or go to church, they ignore you completely.
10. Developers are just out to make money. They use the cheapest materials and charge as much as they can for properties.
11. Do you know why new-build houses have just a ten-year warranty? Because developers know that after ten years things start going wrong, in which case house owners are no longer covered and have to pay out themselves. It's a fact.
12. I bet most new houses in villages, especially on the coast, will be bought by the rich as second homes; their 'escape to the country.'
13. The smell of silage farmers put on their fields is awful. If people buy a new-build house in a rural village, they'll regret it.
14. If the development goes ahead, think of all the extra traffic, like trucks and bulldozers and so on, and the noise and dirt and pollution that will cause. And the more new houses there are, the more cars there will be on local roads.
15. It's expensive to live in a village. Not only do village stores and farm shops charge rip-off prices, but most new residents will need to commute to work, meaning their petrol bills will shoot up.
16. Surely everyone should have the right to own a home. If a developer builds some small houses that people can afford, what's wrong with that?
17. The population of this country is growing, so more houses are needed all the time.
18. I think people should pay a tax if they want a second child, which goes up for each extra child they have.
19. In the same way that the right to life is a basic human right, that should apply to any potential life too. Imposing any penalties on people who want to have children is morally wrong.

20. In the good old days there used to be some houses owned by the council that ordinary working people could afford to rent. Where have such houses gone now – the 'right to buy' policy means they've all been sold off and cash-strapped councils can't afford to replace them.
21. If the building of new houses isn't stopped now then this country will be bursting at the seams!
22. Yes, and who'll be at the top of the list for new houses? People coming here from overseas, that's who. Or parents with loads of kids claiming huge benefits and living off the state.
23. You get lots of cyclists and horse riders on country roads. More houses mean more cars, which means more accidents.
24. Lots of people work from home these days, so fewer people will need to commute. Besides, as electric cars become more popular there'll be less pollution from petrol and diesel.
25. My Dad's friend has got an electric car. It's white.
26. I agree with your point and I think you're very intelligent to have made it.
27. Low-cost housing is all very well, but you need such a huge deposit these days that some people will never get on the property ladder.
28. Only fools would agree with more house-building in villages.
29. If people have grown up in a village, there should be some way of making sure they can stay there if they want to.
30. Build, build, build! Soon, the whole country will be under concrete.
31. What about all these shops and offices closing in towns and cities as businesses fail – couldn't they be converted into flats?
32. Why are flats called flats anyway?
33. Put your money in bricks and mortar my dad always says. He and Mum have made money on every house they've sold.
34. The building society we use says that house prices will fall, making any house more affordable.
35. The more people that want to live in a village, the more house prices there will rise.
36. If new dwellings were built underground, then such developments wouldn't be an eyesore. I think underground towns would be really cool.

Ask children to think of any other comments, including ones that use the rhetorical tactics mentioned previously. This will add to the richness of the discussion. Another technique is to create a 6x6 grid of the comments. Use dice rolls to choose a comment at random and ask the class to analyse it in light of the rhetorical techniques listed earlier.

Ask children to frame their responses to comments in the form of questions as far as they can. So, for example, for comment 3 – I read an article recently which said that such large housing developments cause crime in the area to increase – questions could include; 'Where was this article?' 'What else did it say?' 'Is the writer an authority on the subject?' 'Where did the writer get the information about rising crime?' and 'How does the writer know that the information is accurate?'

Generalised Opinions

The same critical awareness can be brought to bear on generalisations (see page 59). So for example, what questions could be asked of someone who says that 'people on benefits are scroungers'?

Note too that many generalisations are controversial and emotive. As such, it's important that children who are learning questioning and critical thinking skills should not get drawn into the emotional tangle when exploring a generalised opinion. And, as previously mentioned, an important part of the ethos of having a discussion or philosophical enquiry is that it's OK to challenge an opinion but quite wrong to disrespect the person holding that opinion, however strongly you disagree with it. Even so, the same emotional charge that can lie behind a viewpoint might make it impossible to conduct a reasonable discussion: there have been a number of occasions when someone has reacted angrily (or maybe defensively) when we've asked a neutral question such as 'why do you believe that?' or 'why do you feel that way?' In such cases, we think it prudent to back off and let such people just get on with it.

A variation of the emotional charge using 'therefore' cropped up in something an acquaintance of Steve's once said; viz. 'I think, therefore, I reject the Almighty.' This implies that if you accept God then you don't think, which is disrespectful to the millions of people with religious beliefs, many of whom will have thought deeply about their beliefs and not succumbed to what is patronisingly called 'blind faith'. Further, dogmatic atheism that hasn't been thought about is equally 'blind'. What Steve wanted to do was ask my acquaintance, 'So what else has made you reject the Almighty?' But knowing that this man was a staunch and dogmatic atheist, he decided to let it go. As Jonathan Herring advises in his 'How to Argue', sometimes arguing is just not worth the time and effort. Or, as the actor Robert Benchley (attrib.) said, 'Drawing upon my fine command of the English language, I said nothing.'

Activity: Assumptions and Dubious Connectives

Sometimes opinions, not just generalised ones, are based on assumptions that are then spuriously backed up by connectives such as; because, like, so, therefore it follows. Although these words indicate reasoning, such

Figure 6.1 This image prompts children to ask questions about what might be going on between the characters in the picture.

reasoning can often be shaky. Show children these examples, based on Figure 6.1, to illustrate the point.

The man must be warm because his necktie is loosened and he isn't wearing a jumper.
There is snow on the windowsill; therefore, it's nearly Christmas.
If the car belongs to the lady, she must be rich because a car like that is expensive. If it belongs to the man, then he must be rich.
The woman isn't wearing a wedding ring so she must be single.

If any children have noticed that there's no snow on the car, ask them to speculate why this may be so.

The picture can be used in other ways. Once details of the scene have been noticed, encourage a three-step approach to self-questioning –

Based on what we've noticed, what do we actually know?
What do we think we know?
What questions could we ask to find out more or to be sure?

This more measured approach makes it easier to notice assumptions. Also, the more children build it into their thinking skills repertoire, the more likely they are to spot assumptions in what other people say.

The image can also be used to help children come up with alternative scenarios and practise speculative or 'maybe' thinking (page 28).

So is the man's tie loosened because he's warm? Or could it be that he's just come home from work and had just taken off his jacket and loosened his tie when the phone rang?

We think we know that the people in the picture know each other because they're waving at one another. Or could it be that the woman passing by has noticed the hazard lights blinking on the car and, assuming it's the man's, is trying to attract his attention?

But if they do know one another, could it be that they've had an argument? If they're married, maybe the woman has taken off her wedding ring as a symbolic gesture and is giving the man a 'to hell with you' gesture while he holds up a placating hand.

This can be taken a little further –

The person outside the house might be a man in disguise (for some reason).
The object over the 'woman's' shoulder might not be a bag. What else could it be?
Maybe someone else in the house loosened the man's tie.

Finally, ask children to use their imagination to do some 'multisensory thinking': that is, invite children to think about what colours there would be in the picture, what sounds and textures. Have them imagine they can step into the house and notice, say, the smell of the man's aftershave lotion or the aroma of food cooking on the stove. If children are working in pairs or small groups, they can prompt responses by asking questions and then comparing answers – 'So what colour is the man's tie in your mind? Red. Oh, mine's green because my favourite colour is green.' Bear in mind though that sometimes there's no graspable reason for an imagined impression: the child who imagined the red tie might say that he doesn't know, it was just how it came to him. This is perfectly acceptable.

Of course, different children will create different impressions: there are no right and wrong answers in this activity, though if an impression is silly or outlandish, then rather than disrespect the child's idea, ask him to think about why the man's hair is green, for instance, or why the girl starts to do a ridiculous dance in the street. One way of framing this is to say, 'If you chose to use this idea in a story, would it make the story better and, if so, how?' This approach avoids the adult imposing her own views on the child but instead encourages the child to be discerning and discriminating in whether to use ideas or not. The mind is wonderfully creative and all ideas are precious, which is why if a child chooses not to use the green hair or ridiculous dance ideas, rather than discard these suggest a personal or whole-class 'ideas journal', where ideas not used now are recorded for possible use later. This helps children to feel that what they think is valued, rather than anyone feeling put down by being forced or persuaded to scrap ideas they've had.

Finally, if the multisensory thinking activity is run a number of times, many children will find that their imagined impressions become more detailed and vivid, both when they are planning creative writing of their own and also as they read or listen to stories and poems written by others. Simply source some black-and-white pictures, such as Figure 6.1, and run the activity as a 'mind warm up' at the start of a lesson. We go into this use of the imagination in much more detail in 'Visualising Literacy and How to Teach It' (see Bibliography).

Colourful Language

Jonathan Herring, mentioned previously, advises using such language in arguments (where the aim is to gain the upper hand and win), but it's not appropriate in discussions, where the aim is to explore an issue collectively and collaboratively. However, they may begin to creep into a discussion so it's useful for children to be able to recognise such persuasive moves. . .

Analogies

This includes the use of both similes and metaphors, which themselves may be exaggerations. They can sometimes be used to attack the person rather than challenge a viewpoint. Examples include –

Steve, you're like a lapdog agreeing with everything Tony says.
Your reasons are like watery soup, thin and unsatisfying.
Arguing with you is like hitting my head against a brick wall.

Intensifiers

These are used to strengthen a point. Common general examples include very, really, absolutely, totally and a lot. You often find intensifiers in advertisements which universally want to persuade you to buy a product or react in a certain way. So a kitchen cleaner might 'wipe out' germs or can be used to 'blitz your worktops clean', 'destroy bacteria' or 'win the war on dirt.' As an activity, show the class some suitable adverts and ask the children to look out for other examples.

Nuances of Language

Is someone who demonstrates outside Parliament a concerned citizen, a participant in the protest, a noisy protestor or a potentially disruptive or dangerous activist? Is nuclear energy clean and efficient or is it the road to Armageddon (notice the intensifier-metaphor here)? Again, as children become more aware of these in a discussion, they can avoid being persuaded by the underlying viewpoint or use less emotive language to state their views.

Noticing tactics such as these feeds into the whole ethos of the clarity of language, which is an important aspect of critical thinking and incisive questioning. See also the 'Computer in the Box' activity on page 70.

Summing Up So Far

Critical and creative thinking, including their application to effective questioning, involves an attitude as well as a raft of mental abilities. We've touched on some of these throughout the book, but to sum up, and in preparation for the next section, notice which children and to what extent display the following characteristics –

A good sense of humour. This goes hand in hand with a willingness to stand back and not get emotionally involved in one's own strongly held views or those of others. Assertiveness in making a point need not involve aggressiveness to any degree. All other participants in a discussion or enquiry must be respected, no matter how robustly someone's opinions are challenged.

Playfulness. This takes many forms. Playfulness lies at the heart of creative thinking by linking previously disparate ideas and the preparedness to look at things in as many ways as possible – in other words, playing with ideas. And in terms of critical thinking and questioning, the same kind of mental flexibility allows one to explore an issue by coming in from a number of different angles. Aside from that, having ideas and exploring topics should be enjoyable. Fun in learning makes what is learned more memorable – It was the philosopher Plato who wrote that all learning has an emotional base. We take this to mean that learning equates with understanding; with grappling with ideas (evaluation and synthesis in Bloom's Taxonomy of Thinking, page 17), rather than just the recollection of facts.

A healthy resilience to setbacks, which might mean that others don't understand or accept someone's views; that a sought-after fact can't be found, or that one fails to understand particular ideas or information. This is the other side of the coin to one's willingness to persevere in the face of difficulties.

Independence of judgement when it comes to evaluating ideas. This trait is closely linked with the ability to question ideas and make up one's own mind rather than just going along with the crowd or bowing to authority.

All of this builds towards an increasing tolerance of ambiguity and uncertainty and a dampening of the urge to want the right answer right now. This becomes particularly important in a philosophy session, where no conclusions may be reached or where a conclusion takes the form of a raft of further questions rather than any clear-cut answers.

As children tackle ideas in this way, their confidence and self-esteem are likely to grow, and by that we mean how a child estimates himself. As the German educator Kurt Hahn has said, 'Think highly of yourself because the world takes you at your own estimate.' We would add that one's self-estimation should be based on sound reasons and emphatically is not egotism or boastfulness.

A sense of wonder. We've already touched on this (page 4) but mention it again here because it's a sense of wonder that drives curiosity and, further, that wonderment, like having ideas, *feels* good. It allows one to see the world with fresh eyes and a willingness to be astonished by it. Most children are naturally full of wonder ('firstness' as the educationist Margaret Meek has termed it – as though seeing things afresh for the first time), but as they grow they can take things for granted or even become cynical and jaded. We also encourage you to make children more aware and appreciative of the incredible power and flexibility of their own minds, pointing out all of the wonderful things that they can do. In this regard we like to compare the mind to Doctor Who's TARDIS – it's much bigger on the inside than the outside and can take you on the most marvellous adventures in time and space.

And to sum up our summing up, we recommend Max Ehrmann's prose poem 'Desiderata', easily found online.

7 Philosophical Enquiries

The word philosophy comes from the Greek and means a lover of wisdom. We believe that to love wisdom and to explore ideas and 'Big Questions' philosophically requires the attributes we listed in the summing up at the end of the last section. This highlights the point that an enquiry is a collaborative-cooperative exploration of a topic within a formal setting or according to a certain procedure, which we outline below. At least in the US and the UK, the philosophical 'movement' in schools is based on a Socratic approach: the Greek philosopher Socrates felt that philosophy should be by the people and for the people in order for ordinary mortals to live happier and more fulfilling lives. As such, philosophical enquiries in schools and in adult settings in tune with this belief are not highly academic and obscure but rather focus in an accessible way on topics and ideas that have a practical value, even if this amounts to an enjoyable mental adventure that feeds the sense of wonder previously talked about.

There are many books on doing philosophy with children. One of the most compact and easily digested is Jason Buckley's 'Pocket P4C (Philosophy for Children)'. There is also Steve's 'Jumpstart Philosophy in the Classroom'. He also once collaborated with educator Sara Stanley (https://p4c.com/author/sara-stanley/) to produce the book 'But Why?' with a focus on teaching philosophy to young children. You might also take a look at www.sapere.org.uk/; SAPERE being the Society for the Advancement of Philosophical Enquiry in and Reflection in Education.

Since many books already exist in this field and because a detailed explanation of how to set up a philosophical enquiry is beyond the scope of this book, we propose here to give an outline to whet your appetite and encourage you to read more widely if you intend to take the project further. But we feel the need to touch on philosophy for children since it is the ideal platform for honing questioning and thinking skills.

DOI: 10.4324/9781003608714-7

Rules of the Game

A few points need to be made at the outset –

All children have a right to speak and can be encouraged to speak but may choose to remain silent. This might be because some children are shy, are not used to expressing their views or ideally because they are deep in thought mulling over what's being said.

The teacher in the classroom progressively steps back from taking the lead over a number of enquiries becoming the facilitator (one who 'renders less difficult'), then finally a participant on an equal footing with the children. You may even wish to become a silent observer and let the children run the enquiries entirely by themselves. This process of handing over is important: children tend to believe what adults tell them and often defer to adults' viewpoints. The whole point of teaching them to do philosophy is to make them confident and independent thinkers, exploring together within what has been called a 'community of enquiry'.

Rather than being a lone candle in the dark, spread the word and encourage children to spread the word about doing philosophy, both in school and beyond. One route is to become a 'Thinking School', with accreditation from Exeter University. Another angle is to establish a philosophy club in school (as well as doing enquiries with your class). Such a club invites any pupil or staff member to come along, while some clubs that we have helped to establish even sent letters of invitation home to parents who, in some cases, turned up and joined in. In one school, the teacher in charge of the club decided to run a philosophy 101 course where anyone who was thinking of coming was invited along to learn the basics, priming them to launch into full-blown enquiries if they did, in fact, join. The 101 course was repeated periodically to cater for new intakes and for children already in the school who wanted to join now but hadn't come along to the earlier 101 courses.

Obviously, unless 'philosophy time' is built into the school curriculum, it will have to be done at lunchtimes, this being the most common model that we have come across. Depending on the enthusiasm of all involved, such lunchtime clubs can be run on more than one day of the week, with enquiries going on beyond a single session if necessary.

Getting Started

We've mentioned that a philosophical enquiry follows a definite procedure, which is –

As far as possible, have the children sitting in a circle. Not only can they all see everyone else, but the circle symbolises the fact that they are all equal: no one is sitting in a special place. You as a facilitator may want to sit in the circle too, but remember to guide with a light touch and not dominate the conversation.

One or more thinking games serve as a warmup to the enquiry proper. Many examples can be found online. You may want the children to work individually, in pairs or in small groups, spending five minutes or so airing their thoughts before reporting back to the class. The aim is not necessarily to come up with definite answers or conclusions – indeed, some children might admit that the issue is deeper and more complex than they first thought and that they haven't arrived at a conclusion.

Warmup games that have worked well for us include.

Activity: Testing the Limits

For example, suppose you found a wallet in the street containing £100 and nothing else. Would you keep the money, take the wallet to a police station, donate the cash to charity or do something else? Would you do the same thing if the wallet also contained an address? What would you do if there was also a picture of an elderly person? What if the picture was of a well-dressed person standing proudly beside a very expensive car with a mansion in the background? What would you do in each case if the wallet contained £500? What about £1000?

If you decide to keep the money, think of a few reasons to justify your actions. These reasons can be made up. So you might say, 'My grandma is ill and the money will go towards getting some private health care quickly', even if you don't really have a grandmother. Rank each reason on a 1–6 scale, with one being a very weak reason and six being a strong reason, even if it's not ethically sound.

Note: Brief discussions of the 'Lifeboat Dilemma' and the 'Trolley Problem', pages 102 and 109, can also serve as warmups.

Activity: Wrestling with Abstract Concepts

The scenarios are about moral values and the difference between right and wrong. Keeping the money to pay for a grandmother's health care shows compassion and concern, but it is still morally wrong. You can extend the 'testing the limits' activity by asking children to discuss what 'good' means in this context. Take it further by using the word in a number of different ways and discussing what it means. So we talk of a good book, a good cry, a good meal, a good friend, etc. One way of tackling the activity is to encourage the children to come up with synonyms for good in each example. Other abstract concepts we've used include happiness and other emotions, plus the concept of 'emotion' itself. Build the concept into some questions for discussion. For instance –

What is an emotion?
How many emotions can you think of?
How can you tell a positive emotion from a negative one?

Can any of your negative emotions be beneficial? For instance, feeling fear might help you to keep out of danger, while experiencing anger might let you get something off your chest so that you feel better afterwards or it might indicate that you feel strongly about an issue.

Can any positive emotion be 'wrong'? For instance, if you feel happy at somebody else's misfortune, somebody who's harmed you in some way perhaps, is it wrong in any way to feel that happiness?

Three wishes. Simply put, if you had three wishes, what would they be and why? By the way, you're not allowed to wish for more wishes.

'Would You Rather Revisited' (see also page 7).

This is a commonly used warmup; an apparently simple enough game but one that really tests children's thinking. So, would you rather be very rich or live to a ripe old age in good health? Would you rather have a superpower or be really popular with everyone you meet? Would you rather be able to read someone's mind or put your mind in someone else's body? Would you rather be able to see into the future or be able to teleport your body to anywhere in the world? The website www.twinkl.co.uk/resource/t2-roi2-p-3-would-you-rather-ice-breaker-challenge-cards has plenty of examples that are suitable for children.

Present the Stimulus

This can be just about anything; a story, a picture, a video clip, an object, a piece of music, etc. As children become more familiar with doing an enquiry they're likely to find it easier to use a stimulus to come up with some 'juicy' suitable questions. So, for instance, if the stimulus was a stone, a good question would be, 'What does it mean to be alive?' If the stimulus was a picture of a battle, questions might be, 'Is war ever justified?,' 'What is courage?' and 'Can it be right to refuse to fight in a war in defence of your country?'

Thinking Time

Give the children ten minutes or so to reflect on the chosen question and write down some words that would help them to explore the topic further. Once these keywords are written, organise the children into small groups to share their thoughts.

Question Making

Each group then writes what they regard as the best question on a piece of paper and places it in an open space on the floor. Children then vote on the question they want to explore: there are various ways to vote (again, see Buckley's 'Pocket P4C'), but we normally ask children to go and stand by their preferred question. The question with the most votes is the one used for the current enquiry, though the others can be saved for future sessions.

First Thoughts

The group that came up with the chosen question now has the opportunity to say anything further about it. The facilitator may invite other children to contribute their initial thoughts at this stage.

The 'Meat' of the Enquiry

This is the heart of the process, where children probe more deeply into the topic, using a number of tactics or 'moves' to enable this, as explained in what follows. As mentioned earlier, every child is invited to speak but some may not wish to contribute for any reason. Our preference is for children to hold a hand out, palm upward, if they want to speak. This distinguishes the enquiry from the hands-up used in other lessons. And for us it also symbolises an attitude of open-handedness, of ideas and opinions freely given.

We found in one class that a particular child was very insistent about speaking, thrusting his hand out to arm's length and leaning forward on his chair. He had an opinion about everything and our impression was that some classmates were getting fed up with his constant input. Our solution was to present him with some counters. Each time he wanted to speak, he had to 'spend' one of the counters. The advantage of this was that he needed to think carefully about each thing he wanted to say. The disadvantage is that it puts limits on that child's contributions, which some teachers and even other children might think is unfair (though that notion is itself a subject for discussion, of course).

In another philosophy club, a certain child always made long and rambling contributions that slowed down the whole enquiry. Our solution was to make an arrowhead shape with the hands directed at the child. We explained to everyone beforehand that this signal meant 'please come to the point', adding that if contributions were crisp and brief, the topic could be more thoroughly and deeply explored. No one, as far as we remember, found the gesture controversial or unfair.

As the enquiry progresses, the facilitator is there to keep the conversation to the point and ask questions to clarify any obscurity or confusion.

Towards the end of the session, children have the opportunity to offer their final thoughts, although some children may just want to write the thoughts down. Sometimes a conversation is still in full flow when time runs out, in which case it can be picked up again in the subsequent session. One benefit of this is that children have more 'assimilation' time to ponder the topic further.

Once the topic has been thoroughly aired, it's useful to invite the class to review the session, asking the children what they thought worked well and what didn't go so well. The aim is to make future sessions even more effective and enjoyable.

Philosophical Moves

There are a number of ways of encouraging children to deepen their exploration of big ideas and topics and, at the same time, expand the number of ways they can think and question. Before children become familiar with these, make the thinking explicit as necessary by feeding back to the class a particular kind of thinking the participants have demonstrated. You can frame your prompts as questions, a technique that children will also adopt and use.

Clarifying – So how else could we say that to make sure everyone understands? Now that Steve has clearly explained his point, does anyone have anything to add? Who agrees or disagrees, and why?

Conceptualising – So, what's the big idea that all of these points relate to?

Connecting – So what might be the links between those ideas? How can we connect Steve's point with what Tony just said?

Consequences – What might be the result of that? What might happen if this was the case?

Contradictions – We seem to have different opinions here. Can they both be right? Entirely or in part, and why?

Defining – What else can we say to understand that idea more thoroughly? Who can think of any synonyms for that word? Do those synonyms actually mean the same as X?

Distinguishing – So are those examples different at all? Is what Tony said the same as Steve's point earlier?

Evidence – How could we back up that statement? How could we strengthen that opinion/viewpoint?

Examples – Can we think of actual situations where that applies? Can you come up with situations where you think that doesn't apply?

Generalising – Is that always true, do you think? Are there any cases where that isn't true or doesn't apply?

Philosophical Enquiries

Implying – So what can we conclude from all this/from what has just been said?

Reasoning – So what reasons can we think of to support that view? How did you come to reach that conclusion?

Researching – Sometimes in order to develop an enquiry, information needs to be researched or facts need to be checked. A robust procedure is to –

Summarise what's already known that is pertinent to the enquiry.

Be clear about what we need to find out. This might mean making a list of precise questions.

Decide where to go to find the information, being sure to check more than one source.

Decide if any help is needed and who you might go to for that.

Questions, Questions

Philosophical enquiries revolve around questions that address important issues – important in the sense that they are relevant to our lives and/or ideally are intriguing and, therefore, fun to explore. You can explain to the class that there are some questions that philosophers have been puzzling over for centuries. These include –

1. What is consciousness/what is mind?
2. Is there order in nature or is it pure chance and coincidence?
3. Do we have free will?
4. Can you have faith in something without evidence? What counts as evidence?
5. What is real?
6. Why does evil exist?
7. What is beauty?
8. Can we have happiness without sadness?
9. What is intelligence?
10. Who am I?

We're sure you can see how the philosophical moves listed are useful in trying to unpack and probe these questions. In fact, as a precursor to an enquiry, take one of them and go through the list of moves to open up the topic.

As a facilitator, at least in earlier enquiries, you may need to bring children back to the point if the conversation drifts 'off topic', but also guide them into seeing how these big abstract ideas might be relevant to their lives. The question 'What is beauty?' for example, touches upon the issue of body image, self-esteem, the potential damage that social media can do*, the notion that beauty takes many forms and that beauty is not just to do with external appearances. It also links with the question, 'Who am I?' a perpetually intriguing idea that might be especially relevant to young people trying to find their sense of identity.

*Coincidentally, before rereading this section, we came across a BBC News website article pointing out how some social media 'influencers' are promoting skin care products to children as young as eight, but which are only suitable for adults. Unfortunate medical issues can allegedly arise if used on children's skin.

There are websites online offering scores of topics on which to base enquiries, but we advise you to be discerning as to which are appropriate to the age of your children and which may not be philosophical at all. For example, we came across 'How does gravity work?' on one site but to us this is a scientific question that has already been at least partly answered in theory – check out 'gravitons'. We also found, 'Are people of this generation less or more sensitive than people of past generations?' We see problems here. Firstly, there's the question of the false choice, flagged up by 'or'. Maybe this generation is just as sensitive as people of previous generations, although perhaps some people of the current generation are more sensitive and some less sensitive than people of previous generations. But the problem for us goes deeper as we ponder; sensitive in what way? And the question is a huge generalisation – how could we ever know much about the sensitivity of 'previous generations' since we could only assume and infer from any records that have been left? Also, 'previous generations' go back thousands of years. Is there any reasonable way of comparing their 'sensitivity' – whatever that word might mean?

We also came across 'Does observation alter an event?' For us, this is an issue belonging to the realm of quantum physics, the exploration of subatomic particles and forces, so again a scientific matter. On a more mundane level, we might argue that if we were observing – staring at – a person, that in itself might change their behaviour. They might become self-conscious, embarrassed or even hostile. But we hardly think this is the basis for a philosophical topic.

All that said, if you can think of ways of tweaking these questions to make them philosophical, we applaud you.

A related point is that sometimes a philosophical enquiry can become relevant to subjects in the curriculum. While the question about gravity is addressed by science, asking 'Is science good, bad, neutral or something else?' can lead to children's clearer understanding of what science is, the processes and methods of science, which is not the same as the facts and principles that science uncovers. Also, as children become more confident at asking questions within a philosophical context, that tendency is likely to spill over into other subject areas. So if, for example, you happen to mention living things in a science lesson, at least one philosophically savvy child is likely to ask, 'What is life?' And if by chance a question comes along that you can't answer, as we've tried to emphasise previously, a useful response is 'I don't know, but how might we find out?' That attitude links nicely with the ethos of philosophy insofar as when people are confronted by many of its questions, they don't have any right and ready answers. In the philosophy classroom, both children and adults often 'don't know', while the enquiry itself is a joint attempt to find out more and get closer to the truth of the matter.

4Cs

Broadly speaking, the questions that build towards an enquiry and the thinking that goes on within it follow the 4Cs model – caring, collaborative, creative and critical.

Caring questioning/thinking really boils down to taking a sincere interest in what other speakers are saying and respecting their views, even if you don't agree with them – though you are quite entitled to ask for reasons to support the opinion.

Collaborative questioning/thinking simply means that exploring a topic is a whole-class process and a synergistic one, given that the thoughts of many will throw up more insights than individuals thinking alone. But we reiterate that children should not be 'nudged' into taking part if they prefer to remain silent for whatever reason.

Creative thinking/questioning is about making links, using imagination to come up with what-if scenarios, plus the use of metaphors and analogies. For instance, during an enquiry about courage, at one point the conversation stalled until one child said, 'So what if you could give soldiers a pill that got rid of all fear and pain? Would they still be courageous if they then went to war?' This sparked a flurry of opinions (with reasons) and the discussion got back on track.

Sample Enquiry

Here are some of the points that Year 6 children made when exploring this topic. Rather than using made-up names, we've just reproduced the points themselves.

Kickstart question – Are violent video games a good thing or a bad thing? (Note the false choice in 'or'.)
Well, for a start, why decide one way or the other? It depends on what kind of violence. Also, some people might think it's a good thing for whatever reason and some people might think it's a bad thing.
How could it ever be a good thing?

Perhaps some people see violence in video games and feel horrified, which could lead to them becoming less likely to be violent in real life.

On the other hand, people who play such games might get more and more used to it and play more and more violent games.

Facilitator: That's called becoming desensitised, less sensitive, to the violence.

Besides, as long as violence stays in the video games and doesn't spill over into real life, that's a good thing isn't it?

A grown-up friend of mine plays very violent video games and he's a really pleasant person.

What is violence anyway? Where does the word come from?

I checked that earlier. It's a bit confusing, but it comes originally from 'carrying force towards something.'

And in video games to harm the enemy, as in real life.

OK, but if we see a news article about a controlled violent explosion, say to demolish an old building, in a sense that's carrying force towards the building without harming anyone.

I agree, but we're talking about violence in video games.

Professor Jerry Mander from Camford University is an expert on violence in video games and he says it's a bad thing.

What are his reasons for deciding this?

I don't know, but I'll try and find out.

Also, bad in what way exactly – what does he mean by bad?

I think that human beings are violent creatures by their very nature; or at least can become violent. Things like video games and some sports can help people to let off steam.

Do you think all human beings are violent?

I suppose some are never violent and some can become violent depending on the situation, as X just said.

Violence also exists in films, comics and books. And although that's fiction, if violence in video games can have a bad effect, then it can in these other media.

And there's violence in newspapers, on TV news and so on.

My Dad stopped watching TV and reading newspapers once because all the bad news got him down so much.

Facilitator: So we're opening out the enquiry to talk about violence more generally in society. Are you all OK with that? (General nodding)

I wonder – don't you think that's just how the world is? There's violence in people, but animals too can be violent. Nature is violent.

Facilitator: That's really opening out the topic. While I agree with you, I think we should stick with violence in people.

I think there's a link between violence and evil.

But if a burglar was in your house threatening your family and you hit him and knocked him out, even though you used violence, that's not evil, it's self-defence.

Facilitator: That's an interesting example. So we can see here the complex overlap between the concept of evil and violence in humans and the law and justice system. I think maybe we could hold over talking about these until the next time. Now, we have ten minutes left, so split into your usual groups to talk about any conclusions you've reached, whether you've changed your minds about the subject or not, and why. And you can also make notes in your thinking journals if you want to. Then it'll be time for lunch.

I'm having the lasagne.

Note: Steve also looks at violence in video games in 'Jumpstart! Philosophy in the classroom', touching on 36 points which he's designed as infoscraps (see page 95), with commentary on each of the infoscraps.

A Note on Discovery Learning

Discovery learning is proactive and problem-centred, with questioning and critical/creative thinking at its heart. It is an educational approach that is thoroughly and robustly advocated in 'Teaching as a Subversive Activity' by Neil Postman and Charles Weingartner (and a book that we recommend in just about every one of our own books). Clearly, it differs from what has cynically been called the 'tell 'em and test 'em' model of learning, although it seems to us that offering children a platform of understanding across the school subject range, in the form of facts and explanations, serves as a solid basis for encouraging children to think and question their way through a raft of topics.

Discovery learning fits in with constructivist theory, which argues that children actively construct knowledge, building new ideas and experiences into their understanding of the world. On a personal note, Steve learned to be a writer *by writing* and even now can't really define a fronted adverbial, the example he uses to symbolise overemphasising grammatical rules in an attempt to make children better writers, rather than creating a range of opportunities for them to learn writing by doing. We use the analogy that knowing the names of a car's engine parts doesn't necessarily make one a better driver. You might argue that if a car goes wrong, knowing how engines work improves the chances of being able to fix it yourself. We invite you to wonder if the same thing holds true for a piece of writing or whether writers develop an individual style and voice by tackling as many writing projects as possible as they simply become more experienced writers.

In the context of this book, a discovery learning approach provides a useful context not just for the ways of thinking we advocate but for the attitude and ethos we've tried to promote for learning and enjoyment of learning to occur.

If you have tried out the activities and techniques in this book, you might well find that children already have a certain understanding of their engagement with information, viz. –

Expanding knowledge and deepening understanding occurs through a long process of asking questions, part of the question-challenge-doubt approach to engaging with information.

The 'truth' in so many ways is often partial, provisional and relative, and supposed facts can be tangled up with opinions presented through a range of rhetorical/persuasive devices. Even more radical is the assertion by the molecular biologist Darryl Reanney in his book 'Music of the Mind', that 'there is no such thing as an uninterpreted fact'. (We go into more detail around this point in 'Understanding the World Through Narrative'.)

Open-minded scepticism therefore is more useful and effective when dealing with information than either naïve gullibility or hardened dogma.

Inquisitiveness, focused through critical thinking and reflective questioning, is a self-sharpening instrument; another example of learning-by-doing.

8 Questions and Life Coaching

Briefly, the aim of life coaching is to help someone identify barriers to their progress and focus their intentions largely through the use of questioning. It's beyond the scope of this book to fully explore the ideas and techniques of life coaching – that would take a book in itself and indeed Steve wrote one some years ago with his friend Simon Percival: 'Coaching Emotional Intelligence in the Classroom'; emotional intelligence being one's ability to understand the feelings of others and notice our own blocks and barriers and overcome them. The roots of such inhibiting behaviours can take the form of limiting beliefs. These may already be consciously recognised, or lie at a subconscious level, though they might become conscious in the form of insights and intuitions as a coaching conversation proceeds.

Life coaching is one of a number of 'talking pathways' to personal development and, as the title of our book suggests, can be undertaken by children themselves (most successfully we think by upper KS2 children and older), working in pairs with the adult(s) in the classroom overseeing progress with a light touch, much like the facilitator's role in a philosophy session. It's also eminently possible, of course, for you to become a life coach yourself. Many courses are available and Steve, having worked with Simon, who is a professional life coach, can reassure you that it's a fascinating subject.

So in this section we'd like to give you a taste of what life coaching looks like and feels like and the kinds of questions a coach might ask. You'll see also that, to some extent, children can ask some of these questions for themselves and of themselves. So for instance, a child having identified a block to progress might ponder these –

What do you want to achieve?
What would it be like once you've achieved that?
How would it help you – what changes would there be in your life?

What exactly does your goal mean to you?
What will you see/hear/feel when you achieve your goal?
How will you know when you get there?

As a testament to the effectiveness of life coaching; while Simon and Steve were in early discussions about our project, Steve mentioned that he'd been having difficulty with three so-far unfinished novels he had been working on. He told Simon that moving towards the end of each felt like 'climbing up a steep hill, the slope of which keeps increasing.' That image itself was a limiting analogy. Simon went into 'life coaching mode' asking the kinds of questions listed previously and those in what follows and after only ten minutes, Steve felt completely differently about the novels and, keeping Simon's deadlines in mind, went on to finish all three (whether they're any good or not is a different matter). There had been a definite shift in his attitude.

We think that from the point of view of the 'coachee' it's important to be open-minded with oneself and frank and honest with the coach. As such, there needs to be a positive relationship – a rapport – from the outset and trust plus, in our opinion, a degree of lightness and indeed humour even if barriers are serious and currently very inhibiting. That's why we wanted this section to come towards the end of the book because our intention is that children, having worked through previous sections, will now be equipped with the thinking and questioning skills, the creativity and the willingness to work with others to undertake a life coaching conversation.

As an adjunct to and preparation for a coaching session and by way of giving a child the opportunity to look at things from another angle, these questions may be considered, focussing awareness on the 'positive now' –

What is good about now?
What in life makes you smile?
What do others like about you?
To whom would you most like to say 'thank you'?
What makes you glad to know a certain person/persons?
What do you like about your local area?

Although it's possible to ask these questions to oneself if someone is looking on the bleak side or feels down, it's easy to think 'Nothing is good about now' or 'Nothing in life makes me smile'. The value then of working with a coach is that she can ask subsidiary questions or offer further prompts to encourage reflection on a question rather than the coachee making a snap judgement.

Coach: What is good about now?
Coachee: Nothing.
Coach: Give it some more thought. Look around if you like. Think about the past few days. Some bad things might have happened, but what is positive about *now*?
Coachee: Well, my Mum gave me a hug when I got home from school yesterday. Thinking about it makes me feel good now. And she was pleased with the mark I got for my English essay. She smiled as she read it. That makes me feel good now, too. And I like all the posters and displays my teacher has up in her classroom, so that makes me feel good, too. . .

Notice that the coach is not trying to persuade or offer examples of her own – listing what makes *her* feel good about now might have a negative effect on the coachee as the child compares his/her situation with the coach's.

An overview that a coach can keep in mind when talking with a coachee is summed up in Figure 8.1 as the Five R's – Rights, Roles, Responsibilities, Rules and Reasons.

Sometimes it helps to deal with a very trivial 'barrier' first as a way of working towards more significant issues. So, for example –

Coachee: I can't finish my story.
Coach: What's stopping you?
Coachee: My pen isn't working.

Right – I have the right to say, 'I don't understand.'

Role(s)	Responsibilities	Rules	Reasons
Learner	To listen to and think about ideas and explanations.	Listen when someone else speaks.	It's better to admit you don't understand early on than to worry later on.
Pupil in a class	To be patient as other people listen and learn.	Show respect for other people's ideas.	Even if I decide that other ideas are not helpful, thinking about them is still part of my learning.

Figure 8.1 The Figure illustrates a helpful attitude in the context of asking questions for life coaching.

Coach: What could you do about that?
Coachee: Borrow another one.
Coach: What's stopping you?
Coachee: I don't know who to ask.
Coach: What could you do about that?
Coachee: Start asking people on my table.
Coach: What's stopping you from doing that?
Coachee: Nothing.
Coach: What if no one on your table has a spare pen?
Coachee: I could ask kids on another table or my teacher...

Of course this is a very simple and apparently easy issue to resolve. However, it may go deeper. The coachee might have said that he's too shy to ask classmates for a pen. If that was the case, how do you think the conversation might continue? And feel free to ask the children for their ideas. It might also be that the coachee has deeper and more wide-ranging limiting beliefs about himself, a subject we'll look at shortly.

Here's an example of a coaching conversation that endeavours to deal with a deeper issue. It's very brief and may appear glib, but we assure you it's not. Sometimes insights and realisations (making something real in one's conscious life) can happen quickly and have a powerful effect, as did Steve's novel-writing conversation with Simon, which took ten minutes. But again, if the coachee had not taken at least a significant step in the right direction after the following short exchange, how might the conversation have continued?

Tip: You or a volunteer can roleplay being the coachee and, again thinking creatively, keep throwing up reasons why a goal can't be achieved, as in Figure 8.2.

Having said that, it's not the coach's job to persuade or suggest; rather, it's guiding the coachee towards greater self-knowledge and creative insights by 'drawing or leading out' the coachee's own reflections on the issue. This takes us to the roots of the word 'education' from the Latin *educare*, meaning to bring out and develop something latent or in potential. As such, life coaching takes a very upbeat and optimistic stance when it comes to helping people. We think that an effective life coach recognises that coachees can become more truly who they are and what they want to be; as we've said, through their ability to think creatively and to maintain a certain faith in themselves that they can move forward.

Taking the next small step, here are questions you can add to the selection on page 147 to prompt a coachee to think further about resolving an issue –

Coach	Coachee
What do you want? Okay, so what is it you *want*? What does 'happy' mean to you? So, what would it be like to be happy at school? When you think about that, what do you see, hear and feel? What is 'great' like? So what you want is to be happy at school, to see all these smiling faces around you, hear the sound of fun and laughter and to feel great, like you're filled with sunshine?	Not to be sad when I'm at school. To be happy at school. Smiling and laughing, feeling like everybody is your friend. I would enjoy lessons and work with different friends; break time would be full of games and fun. I see lots of smiles. And the sun is shining. I can hear lots of chatter in the classroom, excited but not silly, so the teacher doesn't tell us off. There would be laughing and singing at break. It feels great! Like I'm filled with sunshine! That's it!

Figure 8.2 This Figure adds some detail to the kind of interaction that happens between a life coach and a coachee.

- What is stopping you?
- What has helped so far?
- How might/could you do that?
- What *will* you do?
- Who could help you?
- Who could you tell?
- How will you know when you have achieved this?
- How committed are you to achieving this on a scale of one to ten?

Sometimes, something even more immediate than a coaching conversation can effect positive change. We've mentioned the following anecdote in another of our books, but feel it's apropos to recount it here...

In one school, Steve set a creative writing task and after a few minutes, a child came up to him and said, 'I can't do this'. Steve's reply, off the top of his head on this first occasion of its use was, 'Well pretend you can and tell me when you've done it.' The boy didn't argue; he went away and wrote his story. Steve learned later that the technique is called a reframe; presenting another way of looking at and considering the situation. In this case, 'pretend' takes away the stark reality of 'can't': to behave as though something *is* possible, while 'will' is a presupposition of success, an implicit belief that the young writer will complete the task. That 'will' might not register consciously, but the idea of Steve's faith in the writer's ability to succeed will be assimilated and acted upon subconsciously. Try it; it works like a charm.

On another occasion, a child told Steve she couldn't carry out a writing task he'd set and this time he asked her why not. She said, 'Because I'm thick.' Again thinking on the hoof, he replied, 'Well, pretend you're thin and show me the story when it's finished.' Instantly her mood changed: she chuckled as she looked at 'thick' from a different angle, went away and completed the task.

All of this reinforces what we already know: language is powerful. But of course we need to be aware of and alert to the language that we use, as well as notice the language of others, especially perhaps if we're working in the field of personal development. Steve can remember doing a question-and-answer session with a class and one child asked how he dealt with writer's block. He said that he smashed his way through it, adding 'or we could . . . ?' And the children started coming up with ideas –

Jump in a hot air balloon and sail over it.
Strap on a jetpack and zoom over it.
Use a teleporter and appear on the other side of it.
Wave a magic wand and make it disappear.

The point here is that changing the metaphor changes someone's perception and in the field of EI/coaching, we want the change to be something more useful and positive than what we started with. Steve also works as a hypnotherapist and when he talks to clients about the mind, he uses what has been called the 'map of reality'. If you imagine a map, you'll understand, of course, that it's flat. This helps to remove the tendency to use 'depth metaphors'; that problems are deeply rooted or that we'll need to do a lot of digging to get to the heart of the issue. He also explains that we tend to regard time in terms of space, so we talk about long ago, the distant past and far into the future. These are limiting ways of regarding the contents of one's mind. He also explains that on our mental map, and largely at a subconscious level, past experiences are grouped by association and significance. This means that an incident that occurred last week can be closely associated with an experience that happened in early childhood. Such 'clusters' of incidents often reinforce each other and might lead to the appearance of an unwanted behaviour, a phobia or weight problem, for instance.

This is a side issue, but it does highlight the importance of noticing the metaphors people use to think about the way they look at the world and their relationship to it. Note: There is a section on self-talk – the stories we tell ourselves – in 'Understanding the World Through Narrative.'

Dealing With Limiting Beliefs

Limiting beliefs might appear quickly in one's life or be the result of a number of experiences, linked as we've suggested by association or significance, over time. If you'll indulge Steve relating another personal experience – At around age 10, I was put off Maths forever when I took my exercise book out for my junior school teacher to mark. This was his regular way of doing things. He had just taught us some procedure in Maths and then set an exercise. As he marked my first example wrong, his other hand came up and smacked me on the back of my head. I had, of course, got every sum wrong, so I got around a dozen slaps on the head in front of my classmates. I burned with shame. This created an immediate anxiety about getting Maths problems wrong and caused an instant dislike of the subject. I didn't bother with Maths much after that and ended up in a bottom Maths set in secondary school. What that teacher did would these days be called child abuse and reminds me of a common mantra among poor teachers: 'Well, I taught it to them, but they didn't learn it.'

Perhaps a coaching conversation could kindle some kind of interest in me for Maths, but, frankly, it isn't any kind of important issue in my life and I'd much rather put my time and energy into trying to be a better writer.

Figure 8.3 is a template for dealing with limiting beliefs, the next step in becoming an effective life coach.

SMART

This acronym, Figure 8.4, sums up the aspects of the coaching process that make it effective. It has to be said that sometimes a person's goal cannot be attained or that he hasn't yet thought of a way forward. But in our experience, by and large life coaching conversations, or pondering these questions for oneself, often leads to success.

Cycle Questioning

One technique used in life coaching is to put the same question to the coachee a number of times, as in Figure 8.5. As you can see, the coach is gently persistent in drawing out insights and ways forward from the coachee. Sometimes, a first response is not a considered one and can reflect the coachee's current perception of being 'stuck'. Cycling the same question back to the coachee prompts further thought and often leads to what might be called a 'Eureka moment'; a sudden idea about how progress can be made.

Dealing With Limiting Beliefs.

	Identify by . . .	Challenge by . . .	Resolve to . . .
Formation of Belief.	Examining your thoughts and feelings when encountering new experiences.	Questioning the belief that is forming. Examples – • Poor performance in an activity. What do I need to do to improve? How can I achieve this? Was there anything happening around me that affected how well I did? • Negative view of a person. What might have caused him/her to behave like that? What do I already know about this person that does not support my experience? • Negative labelling of a group (racial, cultural, socioeconomic, etc.) based on the behaviour of one/a few. How similarly might a different group behave in this situation? What word or words would I use to describe the behaviour of this group and how could I experience the opposite in other members of the group elsewhere?	Make a list of ideas for improving my performance next time and practice. Change anything in the surroundings that I am able to. Talk to that person in a different situation. Find out more about them next time. Treat other members of the same group you meet for the first time as an individual independent of that group. Avoid pre-judging (prejudice).
Self-talk.	Listening to what the inner voice is saying, at the time or later, about the experience.	Question information (as in the formation stage of a belief) and reframing rigid language (see previous) can fix attitudes. Examples – The teacher *never* picks me. I *can't* play sport. I *always* get the answer wrong. I'm *no good* at working in groups.	Be open to possibilities and be wary of language that closes off these routes.

Figure 8.3 These Figures explore how a life coach might deal with someone whose limiting beliefs prevent them from achieving their goals.

Behaviour.	Noticing (1) when your behaviour towards others is out of character with how you see yourself or (2) when you feel stopped by a feeling from doing something that others can do.	1. Using 'new eyes.' Stop, smile (if appropriate) and treat *now* as the beginning of your contact with this person. 2. 'Becoming' another person to overcome behaviours brought about by personally limiting beliefs. Imagine that you can not only do this activity, but that you are the best in the world at it. Try on the attitude of that person and, again, start from now.	Be the person you want to be. Write a list of adjectives that describe this person, or think of a person who you would want to be more like and write down words and phrases that describe them. Plan how you might realise these descriptions.
Reinforcement.	Watching out for 'just as I expected' thoughts, being eager to confirm labels and stopping paying attention (or simply giving up) during an encounter.	1. Noticing your 'filters' in action. Ask yourself, What did I ignore in that encounter? What evidence was there that did not support my previous opinion? 2. Ridiculing your belief. Write down the negative belief you are tempted to reinforce and then list ten reasons why it is silly to think that.	Assume that people's intentions are good and that they are similar to you – progressing through life, wanting to be happy, seeking to be valued and occasionally misunderstanding others and making mistakes.

Figure 8.3 (Continued)

Components:	Key Questions:	Plan:
Specific:	What exactly will you do?	Main details:
Measurable:	How will you know when you have achieved this? What will make it a success?	Success criteria:
Achievable:	Who will help you? With whom will you share your action plan?	Advocate:
Relevant:	How will this help you to achieve your larger/ultimate goal?	Rationale:
Timing:	When will you do this?	Date (and time?):

Figure 8.4 This acronym reminds both coach and coachee of focussed questions that help to resolve issues and achieve goals.

Coach	Coachee
What's stopping that from happening?	I haven't made any friends at school since I started here, so I'm not usually involved with the laughter.
What would make it better?	To have some friends at school.
Who would you like to be friends with?	There is a group of three girls in my class who seem nice, but I haven't spoken to them yet.
What *could* you do?	Speak to them.
How might you go about doing that?	Well, I could go over and talk to them.
Good. What else?	I could ask if I could join in with their games at break.
Good. What else?	I've noticed they like running-around games, so I could tell them about a game we used to play at my old school that they might not know.
Good. What else? Just tell me three more.	I can't think of anything else. Well, they all play for the school football team, so I could go along to practice.
Good. What else?	Beth lives near me. I could ask her if she wants a lift to school.
Good. What else?	I really can't think of any more.
That's fine. You've done really well. You've come up with five ideas. Which of those appealed to you most?	Going to football practice. It doesn't feel as scary as the others and I think I might be quite good at football.
What *will* you do?	It's on a Monday night, so I'll check with my parents and then give it a go.
What will you do to make friends while you are there?	It will be easier to talk, so I'll just make sure I find the opportunity.
Great, so tell me what your plan is as you write it down on your SMART sheet.	• I'm going to go to football practice on Monday night and will talk to the girls and, hopefully, get on well with them (specific and measurable with timing). • I'll tell my parents what I'm doing to make sure I don't get cold feet (achievable). • If we become friends, it will move me very close to my overall goal of feeling happy at school (relevant).

Figure 8.5 This life coaching technique requires the coach to 'cycle back' the same questions to the coachee in order to draw out more insights.

How Did It Go?

In our experience, life coaches are optimistic that their techniques will lead to success, especially since coachees are usually highly motivated to effect positive changes. This is particularly apparent when a coachee is willing to pay a fee to employ a professional life coach for his services. In a school setting, as with establishing the protocols to carry out philosophical enquiries, it's best to start small and simple, introducing and practising techniques within the ethos of mutual respect and support. It's reasonable to say, we think, that we all have issues we'd like to address, problems we'd like to solve and goals we'd like to achieve. As and when this happens, it makes sense to look back and reflect on the extent of our success with the following questions –

- How did it go?
- What worked well?
- What could have been better?
- What did you learn?
- What will you do differently next time?

If you encourage children to reflect in this way after a process of change or problem-solving, prompt them both to add questions to this list and to apply them also to other classroom procedures such as a discussion, an enquiry, or any other aspect of their learning.

Question Checklist

By way of summarising some of the questioning techniques explained in this book, encourage children to reflect on the questions they ask by considering the following list, which can most usefully form a permanent display in the classroom –

- Have I framed the question accurately to discover what I actually want to know?
- Could I ask the question differently, and what effect might that have?
- Are there any other questions arising from my first question?
- What resources will allow me to answer my question(s)?
- How can I use the answer(s)?

Endwords

The molecular biologist Darryl Reanney said that 'each time we learn something important, something we did not know before, we change: the person that asks question B is not the person who asks question A.' Questioning is rooted in curiosity and rationality, the very opposite of gullibility and naiveté: being able to ask searching and relevant questions protects us from being taken in by opinions without foundation, persuasive tactics and shaky reasoning. We stand more securely in a world awash with opinions, biases, misinformation, relative 'truths', inaccuracies and outright lies. The ability to ask questions is a fast-track road to becoming more educated in the truest sense of the word, for as the philosopher Plato said, 'To wonder why is the beginning of all knowledge.'

Author Note: Another technique Steve has developed that is useful for prompting children to ask questions is something he's called a dice journey. Here, small groups of children using counter flips and dice rolls, work on a large sheet of paper, think of a theme or basic story idea, and talk/question their way through the adventure, drawing and annotating the story as they go – many of the activities in Section 4, 'Questioning and Creative Writing' would help them with this. He introduced the technique in 'Visualising Literacy and How to Teach It' and had intended it as a section in 'Question Quest'. However, the idea has evolved much further, and he hopes in the future to publish it as a book-length project in itself.

Bibliography

Alexander, M. *The Earliest English Poems*. Harmondsworth, Middlesex: Penguin Books, 1970.
Alexander, M. *Beowulf*. Harmondsworth, Middlesex: Penguin Books, 1977.
Asimov, I. *Words of Science*. London: Book Club Associates, 1974.
Barfield, O. *History in English Words*. Great Barrington, MA: Lindisfarne Press, 1985.
Barnes, D., Britton, J., Rosen, H. & The London Association for the Teaching of English. *Language, the Learner and the School*. Harmondsworth, Middlesex: Penguin Books, 1971.
Berger, W. *A More Beautiful Question*. New York: Bloomsbury, 2014.
Bierce, A. *The Extended Devil's Dictionary*. London: Penguin, 1989.
Bowkett, S. *Jumpstart! Philosophy in the Classroom*. Abingdon, Oxon: Routledge, 2018.
Bowkett, S. & Hitchman, T. *Visualising Literacy and How to Teach It: A Guide to Developing Thinking Skills, Vocabulary and Imagination for 9–12 Year-Olds*. Abingdon, Oxon: Routledge, 2022.
Bowkett, S. & Hitchman, T. *Understanding the World Through Narrative*. Abingdon, Oxon.: Routledge, 2024.
Bowkett, S. & Percival, S. *Coaching Emotional Intelligence in the Classroom*. Abingdon, Oxon: Routledge, 2011.
Bragg, M. *The Adventure of English*. London: Hodder & Stoughton, 2004.
Brunvand, J. H. *The Vanishing Hitchhiker: Urban Legends and Their Meanings*. London: Pan Books, 1983.
Brunvand, J. H. *Curses! Broiled Again!* New York: W. W. Norton & Company, 1990.
Brunvand, J. H. *Be Afraid, Be Very Afraid: The Book of Scary Urban Legends*. New York: W. W. Norton and Co., 2004.
Buckley, J. *Pocket P4C*. Chelmsford: One Slice Books, 2011.
Bullimore, T., Conrad, H., Niederman, D. & Smith, S. *Whodunnits: More Than 100 Mysteries for You to Solve*. London: Sterling Publishing, 2008.
Civardi, A., Hindley, J. & Wilkes, A. *Detective's Handbook*. London: Usborne Publishing, 1979.

Clegg, B. *Are Numbers Real?* London: Robinson, 2016.
Clegg, B. *Dark Matter & Dark Energy: The Hidden 95% of the Universe*. London: Icon Books, 2019.
Cohen, M. *101 Ethical Dilemmas*. London: Routledge, 2004.
Dillon, J. T. *The Practice of Questioning*. London: Routledge, 1990.
Eckwall, E. *The Concise Oxford Dictionary of English Place-Names*. London: Oxford University Press, 1981.
Gardner, W. H. *Gerard Manley Hopkins: Poetry and Prose*. Harmondsworth, Middlesex: Penguin Books, 1970.
Law, S. *The Philosophy Files 1 & 2*. London: Orion Children's Books, 2002 & 2003.
Lockyer, S. *Hands Up*, 2015. www.teacherly.org/.
Magnus, M. *Gods in the Word*. CreateSpace Independent Publishing Platform, 2010.
Marshall, M. (Ed.). *Human Origins*. London: John Murray Press, 2022.
Morgan, N. & Saxton, J. *Asking Better Questions*. Markham, ON: Pembroke Publishers Limited, 1994.
Opie, R. *The 1950s Scrapbook*. London: New Cavendish Books, 1998.
Paton Walsh, J. & Crossley-Holland, K. *Wordhoard: Anglo-Saxon Stories for Young People*. Harmondsworth, Middlesex: Penguin Books, 1972.
Postman, N. & Weingartner, C. *Teaching as a Subversive Activity*. Harmondsworth, Middlesex: Penguin Books, 1972.
Priestley, J. B. *Man & Time*. London: Bloomsbury, 1989.
Reanney, D. *Music of the Mind: An Adventure into Consciousness*. London: Souvenir Press, 1994.
Reps, P. *Zen Flesh, Zen Bones*. Harmondsworth, Middlesex: Penguin Books, 1980.
Rockett, M. & Percival, S. *Thinking for Learning*. Stafford: Network Educational Press, 2002.
Sheldrake, R. *The Science Delusion*. London: Hodder & Stoughton, 2012.
Stanley, S. & Bowkett, S. *But Why? Developing Philosophical Thinking in the Classroom*. Stafford: Network Educational Press, 2004.
Stock, G. *The Book of Questions*. New York: Workman Publishing, 1987.
Stock, G. *The Kids' Book of Questions*. New York: Workman Publishing, 2004.
Thompson, M. *Teach Yourself Philosophy of Mind*. London: Hodder Headline, 2001.
Vardy, P. *The Puzzle of Evil*. London: Fount (HarperCollins), 1992.
Wells, H. G. *The Time Machine*. London: Pan Books, 1968.
Wolf, F. A. *Parallel Universes: The Search for Other Worlds*. London: The Bodley Head, 1988.
Woodlander, D. *How Our Language Grew*. London: Collins Educational, 1989.

Index

Abbott, J. (educationalist) xii, 16
abstract concepts 37, 58, 93, 137
agreement line (to mark degree of
    agreement/disagreement) 105
ambiguity 17, 25
analogies 132
assumptions 44, 129

Barnes, D. (educator) 6
beauty 92
beliefs 122, 147, 153
brainstorming 24

clarity of language 25
coloured cards to show degree of
    understanding 5
confirmation bias 29
consciousness, continuity of 70
contingent (it depends)
    thinking 14
creativity 31
curriculum pressure 24

debating tactics 101
defining 13, 123
dilemmas 9, 109
Dillon, T. (educationalist) 5
discovery learning 145
dogma 121
dubious connectives 129

education, factory model xii, 29
effective learners, attributes of 17
either-or (false choice) thinking
    118, 123, 142

emotional intelligence 147
ethics 108
etymology 11, 57, 58, 121

facts 98, 121
false choice (implied by the
    word 'or') 123
filmstrip technique activity 75
first lines last lines activity 86

Generalisations 17, 61, 98, 122

Hardy, T. (poet) x, 110
Herring. J. (Professor of Law)
    123, 129, 132
Hill, D. (author) 69, 72, 113
Holt, J. (educator) 30
Hopkins, G. M. (Victorian poet) 47

'I don't know' response 2, 5
if-then thinking 107
ignorance 24, 30
inferring 10
'infoscraps' technique 95
intensifiers (really, very etc.) 132
interrogate the speaker
    activity 111

Keats, J. (Romantic poet) 92
kenning (alliterative poetry) 47
knock on activity 56

learners, aspects of effectiveness 17
lifeboat dilemma (for discussions
    on what's morally right) 102

likelihood line (to mark how likely a scenario might be) 105
limiting beliefs 153

map of reality 152
modelling behaviour 2
The Moon Cannot Be Stolen (Zen parable) 110
moral dilemmas 9
motifs 89
multisensory thinking 131

nonsense words 45

'obserpinions' – an unthinking opinion about something observed 29
odd-one-out game 39
open-minded scepticism 39
opinions 122
'or' as a false choice rhetorical technique 123
originality 4, 33

parable 62
phonosemantics (sound symbolism, linking sounds and concepts) 48
pluralising – having multiple ideas around a question, topic or theme 28
point of view 125
Postman, N. (educator) & Weingartner, C. (writer) 145

question-challenge-doubt as an attitude 29, 59

Rabi, Isidor L. (Physicist) x
randomness 88
red herring 123
reflective questioning 26

reframe (changing the way something is perceived) 151
relevance 15
research skills 4
role play 111

scepticism 121
self-respect 35
sensory cross-matching (synaesthesia) 49
settings 84
Sheldrake, R. (biologist) 44
Ship of Theseus, philosophical puzzle 68
sincere praise 4
snap judgements 149
speculation ('maybe thinking') 104
Stock, G (biophysicist) 9
story dice 91

themes 8, 68
thinking skills, making explicit 27
Thompson, M. (writer and philosopher) x
trolley problem (ethical dilemma) 109
Twilight Zone (science fiction TV series) 67

urban folktales 117

visualising 27

wait time xi
'what if' as a thinking tool 9, 16, 51
Whitehead, A. N. (mathematician) xi
Wolf, F. A. (theoretical physicist) 12
Wolf, M. (Victorian writer) 92
wonderment and curiosity 4, 134
writer's block 152

For Product Safety Concerns and Information please contact our EU representative GPSR@taylorandfrancis.com
Taylor & Francis Verlag GmbH, Kaufingerstraße 24, 80331 München, Germany